Making
Your
Company
Human

Inspiring Others to Reach Their Potential

Se Herall

Making Your Company Human

Inspiring Others to Reach Their Potential

by
Le Herron
with Sherry Christie

MAKING YOUR COMPANY HUMAN:
INSPIRING OTHERS TO REACH THEIR POTENTIAL

FIRST EDITION

Design by Kernacopia, Ltd.

Library of Congress Cataloging-in-Publication Data
Herron, Le (with Sherry Christie)

Making Your Company Human: Inspiring Others to Reach Their Potential – 1st ed.

ISBN 0-9779180-3-3

Library of Congress Control Number: 2006923010

When I was a brand-new second lieutenant in the Army Corps of Engineers during World War II, I was out with troops in the field on a training mission. It had been a hard day, and when the mess line was ready I went over to eat. But before I could be served, an old sergeant took me aside.

"Lieutenant," he said, "when your men have been fed, if there's any food left, then you will eat." And while he was at it he added, "And after all your troops have been bedded down, if there's a place for you to lie down, then you will sleep."

This book is dedicated to that sergeant, who in two minutes taught me a lesson about leadership that has been at the center of my beliefs ever since.

Contents

Acknowledgments

This book represents one man's opinion of how to engage people's hearts and help their talents blossom. The values and beliefs it reflects have been shaped by observation of leaders I respect, my own longstanding belief in human potential, and 24 years of good and bad experiences as a chief executive officer.

Many people helped me form my views over this span of time. I am greatly indebted to them, and to those friends and business associates who have encouraged me to take on this project in order to share my ideas more widely. In particular, I would like to acknowledge my obligation to the following:

The associates over the years at O.M. Scott & Sons (now The Scotts Miracle-Gro Company) in Marysville, Ohio, who inspired me to write the messages included in this book;

John Christensen, my mentor as corporate counsel and member of the board of directors, without whose unfailing support I might not have come to Scotts or survived there;

Bill Bernbach, chairman and founder of Doyle Dane Bernbach (now DDB Worldwide), a truly good human being and consummate New Yorker who loved "the innocence of the Marysvilles of the world";

Ron Cowman, president of Kight Cowman Abram in Columbus, who suggested the title of "One Man's Opinion," making it possible for me to encourage dialogue at Scotts;

Arnold Perl, founding partner of Young & Perl in Memphis and an eminent labor attorney, who was a voice of humanity under sometimes trying conditions;

Dr. Ralph Marcus, past head of Psychological Consultants to Industry in Pittsburgh, who stimulated my thinking on the subject of unlocking people's potential;

Arie Kopelman, President and Chief Operating Officer of Chanel, Inc., who gave me faith that this book was a worthwhile endeavor;

My writing partner, Sherry Christie, who found my voice, and whose enthusiasm in pursuing ideas opened up new avenues of thought;

And my wife, Betty, who bore with me while I struggled to accomplish the task.

Chapter One
Why Make a Company Human?
The key to unlocking potential

Chapter 1
Why Make a Company Human?

Companies are usually viewed as inanimate. They have no self. It's considered high praise to say that a business runs like a well-oiled machine, controlled by a CEO who cranks out earnings every quarter.

But a company is made up of people, not pistons. And in the long run, its success is greatly influenced by how these people think and feel about it.

If they see it as an impersonal machine, the effort they put forth on the job may range from diligent to fair. Some people will contribute just enough talent and energy to get by. Why not? What incentive is there to do more?

Now imagine that they consider their company to be a living thing with a character, personality, and values they understand and believe in. It's hard for anyone to feel apathetic in a situation like this. Invited to use their talents in this spirited environment, people are more likely to respond positively and even enthusiastically. Work can become inspiring, fulfilling, and exhilarating. Nor are they the only ones to benefit. As this excitement and energy spread throughout the organization, the company itself can reap tremendous rewards.

Unlocking personal potential

When you first start work, you may not know much about what your company stands for. Sooner or later, though, you'll recognize that you feel either comfortable or uncomfortable there. The more fully you understand its principles and personality — its "self" — the better you can judge whether or not to give it your best efforts.

Most of us would prefer to work for a business that personifies qualities we admire and respect. Honesty, integrity, trustworthiness, respect, and fairness are the kind of characteristics quality organizations are built on — characteristics that are similar to those of good human beings. When you feel in sync with the company's values, you may become more open and willing to share your talents. There's a good chance you will surprise yourself with what you can accomplish.

Think of what happens when you start talking with a new acquaintance. If you discover that you have a lot in common with that person, you tend to open up more. Hearing your own beliefs and ideas reinforced energizes you. You probably look for ways to expand the relationship with this kindred spirit.

In the same way, it can be liberating to discover yourself in an environment where your beliefs are affirmed and appreciated, where you don't feel vulnerable to being penalized for your views. When people recognize that their company stands for principles they can be comfortable with, and even more importantly admire, it leads to a sense of ownership. The more ownership they feel, the more willing they are to give the best they are capable of. In this process, they help shape the kind of company they want to work for: a community of people who share similar ideals.

The importance of inspiration

As the legendary management thinker Peter F. Drucker has pointed out, the work environment has traditionally been an extension of the family. We all want to feel that we're an integral part of this family — that our thoughts are welcome, our work is valued, and important things are shared with us.

This kind of relationship is frequently found in smaller companies, but it can become more difficult to maintain when a business reaches a critical mass. Sometimes precious little information is given to workers, and that which is given may be finely filtered or distorted. As a result, many people don't know what the company is trying to do or how important they may be to its success, so they end up giving only a fraction of their creativity, skill, and initiative to their work.

The cost in human terms is huge. With their potential hidden away deep inside, these people are deprived of opportunities to grow and expand their abilities. They miss out on the joy of using their talent fully, and the satisfaction of achieving things they never thought possible.

Their companies suffer, too. Struggling to become more profitable, they often focus on slashing costs instead of benefiting from the huge untapped potential that walks out the door every day. This short-sighted approach may lead to layoffs whose ripple effects blight entire communities.

By helping to unlock people's potential, the process of making a company human can create an alternate and more desirable reality. The principles are not very complicated, and they hold true for almost any kind of organization — business, government agency, school, community group, or congregation.

The first thing to consider may seem simple, but it's the foundation for everything that follows. Just why do people work?

Chapter Two

Why Do People Work?

Feeding people's souls

Chapter 2
Why Do People Work?

A working man (or woman) does not live by bread alone.

Money is usually considered to be the primary incentive for loyalty. That's true in a negative sense — unfair pay and other financial benefits can certainly affect workers' loyalty. But fair compensation just brings the company up to the starting line. People rightfully expect proper payment for their efforts.

The misconception arises because "satisfaction" and "loyalty" are viewed as the same thing. They're not. Satisfaction is a way of measuring whether basic expectations have been met, while loyalty is a predictor of how a person will behave. A truly loyal individual may want to keep working at your firm even if a competitor offers higher pay. On the other hand, a company may fail to inspire loyalty even if it offers the highest pay in town. Money is important to people, but it's not the be-all and end-all.   When asked what issues have the most impact on their loyalty to an employer, people worldwide[1] consistently ranked these four issues at the top:

1. Fair treatment at work
2. Care and concern for workers
3. Satisfaction with day-to-day activities
4. Trust in workers

Isn't it amazing? In almost every company in every corner of the world, people agree that the most important rewards of their job are being treated fairly, being trusted, and feeling that their work is important.

Companies that want to retain good workers and build a great organization have to feed people's souls. Some of the required elements are integrity and openness, respect, and appreciation of others' efforts. These intangibles help create a climate in which people can flourish as happier and more productive human beings.

Let's make it clear right now this has nothing to do with working longer hours. What people want, and companies need, is for each hour of work to become more valuable and satisfying.

Fairly sharing risks and rewards

Integrity is probably the most important characteristic that people look for in the company where they work. Since integrity is essentially the same thing in an organization as it is in an individual, most people would probably define it as fairness, honesty, being true to your word, respecting others and treating them with dignity, and being mindful of your responsibility to society and the example you set. Do you act the same way when nobody's watching as you do when you're in the public eye?

The great majority of businesses in this country are fair and ethical. But building the integrity of a company takes many years, and it can't sustain itself indefinitely once the high standards are no longer the focal point. For example, imagine how the workers at a once-proud airline recently felt when they learned that while they were being asked to accept pension cuts, senior executives' pensions were being protected in special trusts.

It's hard to believe that any smart company would choose to treat its workers as mere employees (literally, "those who are used"), instead of recognizing them as a uniquely flexible, inventive, and powerful force in shaping the future. Of course, companies don't make this choice. Their leaders do.

In an increasingly global economy, it may seem inevitable that business leaders would treat their workforce differently than their counterparts did 40 or 50 years ago. Back then, workers' loyalty was rewarded with job security and company-paid pensions. Today, with little assurance of a long-term job or benefits for loyal service, many workers bear more and more of the risk that companies used to shoulder.

Whether or not you like the way the pendulum has swung, it raises the question of whether businesses have provided for their people in other ways for taking on this additional risk. If so, it isn't obvious.

Most people thrive on the challenge, excitement, and rewards of doing their best. In fact, this idea is at the very heart of the American Dream. By making more companies human, we can provide more opportunities for workers to call forth their best efforts.

But this process will succeed only if people feel they are appreciated and treated fairly. That is the task of company leaders.

---

[1]"Commitment in the Workplace: The 2000 Global Employee Relationship Report," Walker Information Global Network and Hudson Institute.

Chapter Three
"Unfair To Workers"
Problems with CEO egos

Chapter 3
"Unfair to Workers"

Any discussion of fairness has to begin with the difficult subject of compensation.

A great deal of harm is being done in organizations where top executives keep taking more while asking workers and retirees to take less. In several cases, companies have compelled the workforce to agree to substantial wage reductions while giving senior managers bonuses and other incentives to stay on board.

The rationale is that in hard times, workers must be willing to sacrifice. But are the workers to blame for the hard times? Why doesn't top management appear to make equivalent (or deeper) sacrifices?

It's no secret that there has been an unprecedented rise in CEO and senior management compensation and benefits in recent years. The first $1 million CEO pay package, back in 1971, went to Harold Geneen of ITT Corporation, at that time one of America's largest companies. I well remember the hue and cry that arose: "No one is worth one million dollars!" In 2004, the *average* compensation of major company CEOs was $9.84 million. How times change![1]

The issue of whether a particular CEO's compensation is deserved is a matter for its board and shareholders to decide. The larger problem is that across the country, workers have fallen way behind senior management in the rate of increases in pay. For example, CEOs earned an average of 12 percent more in 2004, while the pay of the average nonsupervisory worker increased by just 2.2 percent.[2]

The ratio of CEO to worker pay has been widening over the years at a startling pace. In 1982, the average U.S. CEO earned 42 times as much as the average worker. Twenty years later, the ratio was 282 to 1. In 2003, it grew to 301 to 1.[3] In 2004, it became 431 to 1.[4]

Here's another way to look at the disparity in pay raises: if the minimum wage (now $5.15 an hour) had risen as fast as CEO compensation since 1990, our lowest-paid workers would now be earning $23.03 an hour.[5]

Is this rate of increase in CEO pay really defensible? Admittedly, running a company could be considered more difficult now than it was in 1982. But *ten times* more difficult?

Most companies do a good job of judging the financial worth of lower positions. It's time to be more realistic about the relative worth of senior management.

Ego is the culprit here: whoever earns the most must clearly be the best. To make sure everyone gets the message, some CEOs also demand that their contracts include memberships to prestigious clubs, personal jets, yachts, houses and apartments, and so forth. These expensive symbols say, "Hey, look at me! I'm the top dog!"

Adding to the problem are contractual "golden parachutes" that provide a handsome payout if the company fails or the executive is dismissed. Many of today's compensation packages all but eliminate risk for CEOs. In other words, those with the most responsibility for making decisions are hurt the least if they bungle it.

Boards of directors rationalize compensation inflation with the argument that "If we want to attract the caliber of CEO we need, we have to pay this much." Why doesn't someone on the board say, "Wait a minute! How can just one person save our entire company? Isn't it going to take the entire workforce?"

When unfairness makes the headlines

When CEO compensation increases are tied to the price of stock, there is a temptation to boost the stock by doing whatever it takes to meet Wall Street's earnings expectations. Many ethical businesspeople have watched with dismay as a small group of CEOs have bent the rules in pursuit of higher pay — usually with the collaboration of other managers, and often the uncritical support of their boards, investors, and the media. Do these people think the rules don't apply to them? Or simply that they're smart enough to get away with it?

It is extremely sad to see such improper and destructive conduct tarnish the very economic system that creates a standard of living no other country enjoys. The business community should be up in arms about this erosion of ethics. Why aren't we? When accusations of CEO greed or corruption are aired, don't business leaders realize that their workers may be wondering if they too are dishonest?

There are thousands of small and mid-sized businesses and many large businesses run by honorable people who treat workers fairly. The fraud and scandals that have been revealed are an embarrassment to these dedicated, capable men and women.

Many voices are calling out for change. But the solution is not more laws and regulations, which will simply lead compensation specialists to figure out new ways around them. The only way the situation will improve is if there is a groundswell of opinion that this type of conduct is unacceptable in our business culture.

Unless companies act voluntarily, change may be forced upon them. Today's circumstances have some of the earmarks of the 1930s, when the union movement arose in reaction to the excesses of corporate barons like John D. Rockefeller, Andrew Carnegie, and Henry Ford. Resistance to fairer treatment for workers led to ugly scenes of confrontation and violence. However, the unions generally prevailed, with walkouts where striking marchers' placards often read "Unfair to Workers!" Since then, however, many unions have grown to resemble their old foes, hindering rather than helping people to find satisfying work. From 1983 to 2004, union membership shrank from 20.1 percent to 12.5 percent of wage and salary workers.[6]

Now excess at the top is the rule again. While CEO pay escalates, many workers are deeply in debt and living on the financial edge. Something will happen, but what? The old unions have lost their moral authority. Unless the business community takes a stand, it would not be surprising to see a grassroots movement of middle-class workers demand more fairness and accountability in corporate compensation.

A matter of trust

When CEOs are obsessed with maximizing their compensation at the expense of others in the company, the natural result is distrust. Once people see how unfairly the rewards are distributed, they hesitate to give their best efforts. Without a sense of trust and fairness, it becomes impossible to inspire them to share their talents fully.

Accordingly, the ability to unlock the utmost potential of a workforce must be predicated on the highest ethical and moral standards of leadership. This kind of leadership puts one's own needs last — and the needs of other workers first.

---

[1] Pearl Meyer & Partners survey for The New York Times, April 2005.

[2] Ibid.

[3] Matthew Boyle, "When Will They Stop?" Fortune, May 3, 2004.

[4] "Executive Excess 2005," The Institute for Policy Studies and United for a Fair Economy, September 2005.

[5] Ibid.

[6] Bureau of Labor Statistics, U.S. Department of Labor, January 27, 2005.

Chapter Four

Me First!

The nature of leadership

Chapter 4
Me First!

Suppose you get up tomorrow and drive to work as usual. But strangely, the parking lot is empty when you arrive. You walk in the door, expecting the usual cheerful greeting, the busy hum of voices, clicking of keyboards, and ringing of telephones, but the only sound you hear is your own footsteps. No smile welcomes you in the darkened reception area. No voices chatter, argue, laugh in offices or corridors. You look out the window: no smoke rises from the factory stack.

Nobody else has come to work. How much of what has to be done could you do with your own two hands?

Without support, leaders are completely helpless. Unless other people are willing to work with them, there is no hope of great earnings, share-price increases, or business growth. So when the rewards are divided up, shouldn't leaders make sure these other people know how much they are appreciated and valued?

Unfortunately, recent examples of CEO excess show leaders who are at the front of the line with their hand out, oblivious to whether anybody else gets a fair share of the pie. These CEOs have the idea of leadership completely backward.

My eyes were opened to this in an embarrassing way. Soon after being commissioned as a young Army officer near the start of World War II, I came back to camp with my troops, tired and hungry, and got in the mess line. An old sergeant came over and took me aside. I'll never forget what he said.

"Lieutenant," he told me, "when your men have been fed, if there's any food left, then you will eat. And after all your troops have been bedded down, if there's a place for you to lie down, then you will sleep."

This brief admonition has had a more profound effect on me than anything else in my life. In all the business seminars and lectures I have attended, and all the books and magazines I have read, I have never seen a better explanation of the responsibility of leadership.

Those who would be first...

Leadership is not about what you get out of it. It's about what the individuals you are responsible for get out of it.

You can only bring out the full potential of the people in your team, congregation, or workforce if you put their interests before your own. If you have a "me first" mentality, it will be extremely difficult for them to trust you.

If you remember nothing else from this book, please remember that. Whether you think of it as "servant leadership" or "he who would be first shall be last," you have to be able to buy into this philosophy, or else you may as well stop reading now.

Results and rewards

In my rude awakening to true leadership, the "me first" issue was food and sleep. In the case of CEOs with rocketing compensation, it's money, perks, and prestige. For managers up and down the ranks of an organization, it may be personal recognition. These "me-firsters" often claim all the credit for a group project, assuming that sharing the glory will somehow diminish their accomplishment.

But for a leader, getting results is more important than getting credit. That's important enough to bear repeating: *Getting results is more important than getting credit.* When the next challenge arises, people will be more willing to give their best if they can count on a fair share of the applause as well as the material rewards that go with it.

"Me-first" managers should realize that they will reap immeasurably greater personal benefit from putting other people's interests ahead of their own. The gratification of personal ambition can't hold a candle to the pleasure of seeing people in your organization fulfilled by their work. The news of a marriage in your "work family," a first home, or a child graduating from college can provide more joy and pride than any executive pay package, however lavish. To some extent, you have helped people accomplish these things as part of their success.

Personifying your company's character

How does this tie in with making a company human?

There is little value in defining what a company stands for unless its leaders live by similar principles. For example, if a CEO is infamous for humiliating subordinates, how many people will believe the assertion that respect for others is one of the company's core values? As the saying goes, "What you are speaks so loud that I cannot hear what you say."

In this example, people will wonder whether rudeness isn't really valued more than respect. Talented individuals who do believe in respecting their co-workers may conclude that this is not the kind of company they want to work for.

When a leader communicates a set of expectations but does not personally live up to them, it's a variation of the "Me first" mindset. It says, "I think everyone should act this way — except me." If you are to succeed in unlocking people's potential by defining the company's guiding principles, everyone must see that you don't just talk the talk. You also need to walk the walk.

Leadership is not a coat you put on when you arrive in the morning and take off when you leave the office. It's a state of being, a way of life. It affects everything you do and say, whether you know it or not. You may be proud of what the company stands for, or you may be ashamed of it; but either way, you have to live with it inside you. You have to feel it in your gut. You have to live it, laugh it, cry it.

Some leaders are afraid to expose themselves so fully: "If I make a mistake, won't people stop looking up to me?" But unless you open yourself up to others, it's hard to earn their trust. When you are willing to make yourself vulnerable to being unpopular in some quarters, to being proved wrong, even to losing your job for what you believe in, people under your leadership tend to be more forgiving of your mistakes.

And people are the only strength a leader has. When people trust you and are willing to follow you, higher authority has to recognize that it's not in their best interest to remove you. This, not a multi-page contract, is what buys job security.

If you can't see becoming this vulnerable to yourself, the people you're responsible for, and your boss or board of directors, living the company's values may not be a wise choice for you. It can be a humbling experience. But if you're willing to undertake it, the only casualty will be your sense of vanity and ego.

Inspiring the best in people

Wherever you are in your career — CEO, senior executive, junior manager, or business school student — I believe that living the principles we've discussed is critical if you hope to earn people's trust and encourage their talents to flourish. But there is a limit to what can be achieved through personal example. Before people can decide whether to contribute their abilities wholeheartedly, they need to understand not just what you stand for, but what you believe the whole enterprise stands for.

You have a tremendous opportunity to inspire people's potential by shaping and sharing the character of your company. Let's look at a specific way this challenge can be approached.

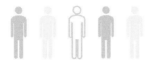

Chapter Five

Shaping and Sharing the Character of Your Company

How to make your company talk

Chapter 5
Shaping and Sharing the Character of Your Company

Every organization has a unique history and personality. If your company's walls could talk, what would they say?

The process of making your company human challenges you to articulate its character — the complex of psychological and ethical traits that distinguish it. Deep inside itself, what sort of place is it? What does it stand for? What are its beliefs? What should it strive to be, in terms of qualities that individuals can relate to and personify? What characteristics did it have at one time that it has moved away from, such as honesty with customers?

To find the answers, listen to people. Seek out workers and retirees, as well as members of the community. What do they think of the company? What do they like and not like? What are they proud of?

If people are hesitant about opening up to you, it means they feel vulnerable. You need to break through to the point where they trust you and are honest about their feelings. It would be great if you could push a magic button to make this happen, but only your actions over months, years, even decades will prove that you can be trusted. If you are new to the company or have been associated with past problems, you'll have to work harder to assure people that speaking painful truths will not harm them.

The good, the bad, and the ugly

Shaping and sharing the character of your company requires you to deal with its negative as well as positive aspects. Perhaps it has outstanding virtues that just need to be more widely communicated. In other cases, the culture may include undesirable qualities such as favoritism or deceit. These characteristics are certainly human, but they won't inspire allegiance and enthusiasm in most people. You may need to explore the company's heritage to find more enduring principles to emphasize.

Suppose a series of mergers has created factions in your organization, leading to apathy among individual workers. By digging into the background of the original companies, you may be able to rally people around a common strength such as innovation or outstanding customer service.

Of course, a program to make your company human is only part of the answer if a problem permeates its very fabric. You may need to use all the powers of a CEO, not just communication, in moving the organization to a more positive place.

Discovering yourself

An important personal benefit follows from discovering and documenting your company's character: you are forced to reveal your true nature to yourself.

What kind of person are you: idealistic or pragmatic? Stubborn or flexible? Logical or emotional? If you are both extremes, when are you each one, and why?

Do you aspire to lead in order to do things your way? If so, what is "your way"? What principles are sacred to you? Why are they sacred? How well do they mesh with the principles that are fundamental to your company? Can you be comfortable living the values your company stands for?

There are a lot of questions here (and even more in Chapter 9, if you are interested). Be sure to take your time answering them. It's better to be confident that you're on solid ground than to rush out with programs and communications that have not been fully thought through. Above all, you must prepare to be scrutinized as an example of what your company is and aspires to be, day in and day out.

When should you start?

Start now.

It's fairly common for CEOs to send memos or letters when the company has problems, such as difficult labor negotiations or the threat of regulatory action. Under these circumstances, by all means go ahead and say the things that need to be said.

But it's much better to start communicating when the company isn't in trouble. People will be more curious about your messages, and more willing to give them an unbiased hearing. Furthermore, if a negative issue comes along later, you will have established a foundation for explaining how it may change the character or focus of the organization. People can then consider whether or not to go against the company's established principles in responding to the problem.

Should anyone else be involved?

It's appropriate to go to your closest advisors before starting a communication program. However, some will probably be reluctant to agree with making yourself this vulnerable. Instead of asking for their approval, you might say, "I have been struggling with this. I feel strongly that it's important for all of us, and believe we all will benefit. Directionally, these are the things I'm planning to talk about. What are your comments?" In the best of all situations, you will find them not only solidly behind you but eager to suggest more possible messages.

What are the best ways to communicate?

Once you have thought deeply about your company and its character, your own circumstances will determine how to use this information to shape the future. The only wrong thing to do would be to withhold it from the people you work with.

Managers often worry about overinforming people. In my experience, that's impossible. We all tend to underestimate what others can contribute when they understand a situation.

If you can meet with the entire workforce, ideally in person or perhaps by videoconference, you might consider giving short talks on various aspects of the company's character. We would not recommend using broadcast voicemail or e-mail, since messages delivered this way are not always received in a timely fashion. Mixed with everyday communications, they can also seem short-lived and inconsequential.

Instead, we strongly support using the printed word for a program of this magnitude and significance. When something appears in print, it is documented for history. There's a permanence to it. For what you want to achieve, there's also the advantage that you can mail your messages to workers' homes. This lets you inform and educate spouses and other family members as well.

What form should these printed messages take? That's really up to you. If you're an informal sort of person, a memo format may feel most comfortable. Signed letters are an excellent alternative if you're striving for a more dignified approach.

After each message has been sent out, you may want to post it on your company's intranet. If the communications are of general interest, putting them up on your external Website will allow you to reach current and potential customers and investors, as well as influential voices in your industry and your community.

How should you say what you feel?

Try to reach deep inside for the right ideas and words. Only by expressing what you honestly believe will you give others in the company the courage to stand up for their own beliefs and ideals.

Overall, it's best if your tone is that of a respectful proposal for dialogue, not a sermon or a harangue. After all, you are not Moses coming down from the mountain with the Ten Commandments. You are merely trying to articulate what you think the company is and wants to be. If these reflections strike a chord, other people may be willing to work with you to fulfill their own needs and desires. As the old sergeant said, you're there to make sure they get fed, not to feed yourself.

If you have difficulty finding the right way to express yourself, it may help to walk through your facilities. Talk with a machine tender on the manufacturing line, a technician in Research and Development, an administrative assistant at headquarters. Try to write your messages simply and directly, as if you were talking with these people face to face.

Getting started and continuing

Once you have identified half a dozen topics that you're comfortable with, write up the first one or two and make your first mailing. Then ask for feedback.

Conversations about a particular message will often lead to an idea for another one. Put aside your preconceptions as you search for topics that are important to people in your company. You will be amazed at how this effort evolves, how diverse the subjects become, and how exciting it will be for you.

It may be a good idea to commit to sending five or six messages before you pause to take stock of the program to date. Some confusion, skepticism, and even criticism are normal. This input can be valuable in fine-tuning the new messages you develop.

In particular, you may hear people say about some topics, "But that's not the way it is now." The answer to this objection is simply "Yes, there's a lot of idealism in my beliefs. What's wrong with that? Even if things can never be as good as we all want them to be, at least we can move toward that ideal."

Even then, not everyone will be eager to jump on board. It's hard to imagine that anybody can be blind to the advantages of freeing up people's potential, but some managers could be unenthusiastic about the program for a variety of reasons. They may subscribe to the traditional view of management in which people are told what to do and are expected to obey without question. Others have too much ego to make themselves vulnerable, or think it's wimpy to show respect for those who are lower on the totem pole. More than a few may be afraid to reveal too much of themselves.

A criticism you may hear from some numbers-oriented managers is that the program won't produce measurable results. But this is not something you run surveys about. Its purpose isn't to produce a statistic for the annual report; it's about feeding the heart and spirit of your company.

You have to commit to this effort over the long term and just keep working at it. If you put a lot of thought into it, the results will be self-evident.

Actions speak louder than words

In communicating to make your company human, the most important rule is to send out a message only if you believe it, can defend it, and are willing to act consistently with your words. When it's written down, it's there for all to see. Be sure you are ready to stand behind it.

If these guidelines seem a little loose, it's because every organization is different. Let your program develop in a way that suits your people and your issues. In the next chapter, you'll see how this kind of effort evolved at a company whose acquisition by a big conglomerate threatened a unique culture and work ethic.

Chapter Six
Bringing People Together
How Scotts blossomed

Chapter 6
Bringing People Together: One Company's Story

When I joined O.M. Scott & Sons, the national manufacturer and marketer of Windsor® Grass Seed, Turf Builder® Lawn Fertilizer, and other lawn care products, it was nearly 100 years old with rich traditions, a greatly respected name, and high ethical standards.

Coming from a company that had nearly foundered on strife between labor and management, I marveled at Scotts' harmonious climate. Its people were known as "Associates" well before this now-overused term lost its true meaning. Most of them came from the surrounding community of Marysville, a rural Ohio town where descendants of industrious German immigrants adhered to a strong work ethic. Many people had a parent or other relative who had worked at Scotts. They had known the company all their lives. Most had never been employed anywhere else.

Equally as remarkable, Scotts made every effort possible to pay its people well and have good benefit programs. These included medical coverage for families, paid vacations and holidays, and pension and profit-sharing plans. In addition, the company provided a multi-acre park with an Olympic-size swimming pool, tennis courts, baseball diamond, picnic areas, fishing pond, and nature trails.

The tide of change began to turn slowly at first, as more and more people were brought in from the outside. I was one myself. Only the fifth CEO of this closely-held company in more than a century, I was the first one who had not been born and raised locally and spent his entire career at Scotts.

Then we were acquired by one of the world's largest conglomerates at that time, ITT Corporation. A $17 billion multinational giant, ITT owned Hartford Insurance, Sheraton Hotels, and hundreds of other companies manufacturing everything from baked goods to telephones. ITT management saw the potential to dramatically increase Scotts' profitability by applying cost-cutting principles that had been used in other acquisitions.

This presented us with a huge new challenge. Much of Scotts' unique nature could be lost if we were pressed into the traditional ITT mold. Our uniqueness was already endangered by the changing composition of the workforce. We had begun to hire a new generation of local workers who often took the company's character for granted. Now we saw that some of the managers joining us from ITT didn't understand or appreciate it.

To protect and strengthen Scotts' character, we needed to make everyone familiar with the company's identity, integrity, and quality. Success in communicating these intangibles would help us not only educate the newer people but reinforce the beliefs of longtime Associates. To my knowledge, this had never been attempted before.

The first step was a giant one. ITT's top management agreed to leave all of Scotts' Associate benefits in place — our pension, family medical coverage, park, and so on — as long as we met profit expectations. This concession was unusual, but I strongly believed that the quality of the Associate relationship was an essential part of Scotts. Going out on a limb to preserve it seemed a worthwhile risk.

Again, it's hard to earn other people's trust unless you make yourself vulnerable. Many of our people recognized that my belief in the importance of Scotts' character made me vulnerable to ITT. I think the majority of them treated me with more forgiveness as a result.

Deciding how to reach people effectively

I was convinced that the better our Associates understood our company's heritage, its fundamental principles, and — yes — its soul, the more open they would become to putting forth their best efforts. The question was how to educate ourselves and, in effect, ITT about the uncommon aspects of Scotts' nature.

Top management was already quite visible and accessible. For example, we maintained an open door policy, took frequent walking tours around the company, and held quarterly meetings to share with all Associates the information released to shareholders. There were many opportunities to share, if only by example, the qualities that shaped Scotts' character.

Our quarterly Jobholder Meetings did become part of the communication process. However, we decided that the core of the program would be a series of letters, which would help us disseminate the messages more widely in both Marysville and New York. It would also ensure that everyone on every level of the company received exactly the same information in a format that let them study it at leisure. Because we valued the support of our Associates' families, who also had a stake in the company, we decided to mail these letters directly to their homes.

The evolution of a company's story

I had used letters before with mixed success. As the newly hired general manager of American Hardware Supply Company (later Servistar), I wrote to jobholders in an attempt to educate them about serious problems with the Teamsters Union. These messages were somewhat helpful, but it's difficult to earn people's trust if you communicate only when the company is in trouble.

By contrast, there were many good things to talk about at Scotts. Many more, in fact, than we were able to imagine at the outset. It started with a list of half a dozen topics, from "the heart of our business" to "price and the customer." Other ideas came as the letters began to reach our Associates. It was like following a trail I had never been on before. Six letters became 10, then 15, then 20. By the time of my retirement seven years later, we had sent 33 letters. (They are included in Chapters 7 and 8.)

As the messages went out, they became a touchstone for all of us, prompting us to examine and take a stand on what we believed in. Some people had been aware of Scotts' guiding principles, but had never seen them written down. Many Associates instinctively felt a connection between these principles and their own beliefs.

What were the results?

Scotts did very well during these years. We expanded into professional turf and nursery markets, developed a new tier of premium lawn products to help smaller retailers compete against mass merchandisers, and established a strategic partnership with a leading European garden products company. We built a second manufacturing plant, a research center, and a headquarters building. All are situated within sight of each other on 300 acres outside Marysville, bringing more than just symbolic unity to a company whose few buildings used to be scattered all over town.

Our financial results were outstanding, as ITT Media Information Manager David R. Allen noted in a Letter to the Editor of *Fortune* magazine:

> *...Scott has shown tremendous growth since it was acquired by ITT in 1971. Between 1971 and 1981 Scott's sales increased by 280% and its net income by some 560%. Scott's growth in sales in the decade preceding the acquisition was only 50% and its growth in net income only 60%...*

> *Under F. Leon Herron, who has been president since 1967, Scott has been a most pleasant addition to the ITT system.*[1]

It was certainly an advantage to have the support of ITT's financial disciplines and resources. But these remarkable results could not have been achieved without the ingenuity, initiative, and commitment of turned-on Associates. Our communications program was an integral part of making this possible.

One measure of the letters' impact is that the Associates in our research division decided to publish them in two hardcover books. In the foreword of the first volume, *Sharing Some Thoughts*, they wrote that the messages "...are a unique and inspirational way of bringing home to all Associates who we are, what the company stands for, and our belief in the importance of fundamental values... So that [they] will be available to all Scott Associates in the future, we in Research have taken the opportunity to reproduce all the letters to date."

An approach that has stood the test of time

The program's most powerful effect has only become evident since my retirement. Many Scotts Associates have never forgotten how good they felt about themselves and their accomplishments during that time. More than 20 years later, I still bump into people who say how memorable the era was for them. Several Associates have said, "You believed in me." One person told me, "You had more confidence in me than I had in myself." Another said, "You led me to do things I never thought I could do."

Recognizing that the company's values were ones they, too, could take pride in, these people unlocked the potential deep inside themselves. Their talent blossomed. And unlike many others who are less fortunate, they experienced the joy of work.

By making a company human, we called forth the best in our own humanity. No club membership, corporate jet, penthouse apartment, or other tangible reward can be more fulfilling for a CEO than this.

---

[1]"Letters to Fortune," *Fortune*, June 14, 1982.

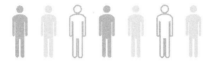

Chapter Seven

The Scotts Letters:
Sharing Some Thoughts

Why are we in business?

Chapter 7
The Scotts Letters

To communicate the unique character of Scotts, the first topics we explored dealt with our heritage, how we do business, and why we do the things we do. The letters in this series, which was titled "Sharing Some Thoughts," fall into two categories: "Who We Are" and "How We Do Business."

"Who We Are"

To some extent, O.M. Scott & Sons created the lawn culture in the U.S. Starting in the 1920s and '30s, when lush, green lawns were the exclusive province of the wealthy who could afford to maintain them, Scotts made it possible for ordinary people to desire and achieve that beauty themselves.

Until then, grass seed was often contaminated with weeds, while fertilizers could be either odorous or toxic to the grass if not precisely applied. With weed-free seed and safer fertilizers, Scotts not only raised the bar in terms of quality and reliability, but also made a beautiful lawn affordable for the average consumer.

Did they create a desire that had not existed before? Far from it. Scotts helped fulfill a natural human longing to be surrounded by green and growing things. Even residents of high-rise apartment buildings cultivate houseplants on their fire escapes. Surgical patients in hospitals heal faster when they are able to look out a window at trees, according to a Pennsylvania study. And to help reduce stress, plant-filled lobbies and courtyards, along with landscaped lawns and groves of trees, are increasingly part of workplace design.

From this point of view, Scotts did not just have a business. We had a mission.

"How We Do Business"

Many companies sell products whose quality and efficacy are not obvious at point of sale: a can of paint, for example, or a computer. However, customers are usually able to judge the value of these products when they begin to use them.

Scotts products are among the very few that are still "phantoms" at point of use. Only days or weeks later is it clear whether the product lives up to the user's expectations. In the meantime, unknown factors come into play, such as timing, weather, and the accuracy with which the seed or lawn product has been applied.

The phantom nature of our products made it essential for our customers to trust us. This is why Scotts offered a No-Quibble Guarantee, Lawn Care Magazine, a Toll-free Hotline for consumer questions, seminars for turf care professionals, and so on. All these services helped encourage customer confidence that our products would do what we said they would.

Some of our people weren't aware of this fundamental difference in the way we did business. Many Associates had not worked anywhere else, while others' experience had never included a company like Scotts. Periodically it was pointed out that our competitors didn't sponsor similar services, so why did we do it? The letters included in this section helped us explain why.

Who We Are

What business are we in?

Some people at Scotts believed the company's business was manufacturing lawn fertilizer and packaging grass seed. When our letters urged them to view Scotts' business as helping customers surround themselves with green and growing things, it opened their eyes and gave them a greater sense of pride and purpose.

Many times, workers are given too little information about what their organization stands for. Without the opportunity to understand and be inspired by its values, they are cheated of a chance to discover the scope of their own abilities. They may still work hard, and if other conditions are favorable the business will prosper. But the loyalty will be missing, and the resilience that keeps companies strong when the going is hard.

What business are you really in? Do your people know? If there have been mergers or a number of new hires, this may well need to be communicated. When your business model has multiple tiers or your products' value is hard to judge, an explanation of the company's purpose can enlighten even some veterans. In any event, it helps everyone become more knowledgeable and may make it easier for them to understand changes that are going on.

With the passage of time, I am more convinced than ever that many companies can benefit from openly discussing the nature of their business with their workforce. On the following pages are the letters that helped define and shape Scotts' character by explaining this aspect of "who we are."

"The Heart of Our Business"

The first of the nearly three dozen letters we sent out at Scotts, this message immediately struck a chord of recognition and pride with many Associates. It also had an underlying purpose: to help managers who were new to Scotts' culture understand that the company was more than sales targets and cost per box of grass seed. Our purpose, the reason for our existence as a company, was to meet one of our customers' most important basic needs.

When you are writing about the heart of your business, it's useful to step back and look at your company from the viewpoint of your ultimate consumer. What service do you provide to him or her? What need do you meet?

 ## The Heart of Our Business

The other day I was having lunch with a friend when an acquaintance of his came up to us to say hello. In the course of the greetings my friend was good enough to introduce me: "This is Le Herron, of O.M. Scott." And then, as we were met with a blank look, he added, "You know, Scott Seed." Instant recognition: "Oh, of course."

I'm sure that's happened to you. You've been introduced as being with "Scott Seed." Or with "Scotts, the people who make Turf Builder." Or with "Scotts, the lawn people." We have a lot of identities. And they make me wince a little, because none of them really gets to the heart of who we are. Or <u>why</u> we are. I'd like to take a few minutes to share some thoughts on that with you.

Scotts is not in business just to sell grass seed. Or Turf Builder. Or any other product per se. We are in business to offer people better ways to surround themselves with green and growing things.

The truth is that our business is rooted in the dreams of nearly every human being... the longing for greenery that is partly love and partly need, a desire for natural beauty that is one of man's fundamental instincts. All we have done is to recognize the limitations of man's ability to fulfill this dream – and help him to make it happen.

And the dream goes on. As the pressures of life increase, the need for greenery, far from being suppressed, intensifies. Our opportunity to grow and to prosper will be limited only by our ability to help people achieve satisfaction. Ten or twenty or fifty years from now our raw material and our finished products may be totally different from what they are today. But the need for our particular capabilities will never disappear, and so our business purpose will not change.

Perhaps we should measure everything we do against the question, "Is it helping someone make their dreams come true?" If it is, then we are being true to Scott's tradition and we can't go very far wrong.

I would like very much, someday, to be introduced "Le Herron of Scotts – you know, the people who help bring you nature." THAT is a wonderful business to be in.

"Lawn Care"

Is there anything that symbolizes your company's relationship with its customers? At Scotts, it was *Lawn Care*, our free quarterly bulletin mailed to lawnowners all across the country.

Predictably, every time money got tight someone would say, "Look how much it costs us to send out *Lawn Care* four times a year! If we eliminated it, we could put a lot more salespeople out there calling on retailers."

At the time this letter was written, Scotts had been educating consumers through *Lawn Care* for 50 years. That was a milestone worth celebrating, and an opportunity to remind everyone why this effort was an important part of our company's character.

Lawn Care

The first issue appeared exactly 50 years ago, on the brink of one of the turning points in this company's history. Dwight Scott and Chid Mills had just made the decision to expand out of the golf course market and start selling grass seed to homeowners. A courageous move, considering that we had a substantial but still expandable 20% share of the golf course seed market at that time, and we didn't know much of anything about consumers. What was even more intimidating was the fact that the consumer didn't know much of anything about grass seed, either.

The genius of these two men, I think, was that they realized the issue at stake wasn't really selling grass seed. The consumer didn't – and doesn't – really want grass seed, or fertilizer, or a control product; what he wants is a <u>lawn</u>. You know, Dwight and Chid could have developed a direct-mail bulletin back then and called it "Principles of Growing Grass" or "Everything You Always Wanted to Know about Grass Seed Germination"... instead, they called it <u>Lawn Care</u>. And I believe that was brilliant. With those two words, they defined this company's business not in terms of products, but in terms of results. They recognized the basic human need for greenery and beauty that is our tie to nature; they appealed to it in words and later pictures; and they explained how Scotts could help fulfill it.

The marketplace has changed in these 50 years, as a result of our efforts. We've educated people to understand that a lawn is something they can create for themselves; we've removed a lot of the "golf course mystique" that surrounded growing healthy grass, and people don't take it for granted any more that they're stuck with whatever scraggly or balding ground cover they may have inherited or caused through error or neglect.

It's a measure of our success at this task that so many other companies have joined us in the market we created, to the point where the consumer now has many dozens of different products to choose from. But as we've been saying, it's not really the products he's interested in; it's how to turn them into a lawn. What should he buy, when should he use it, how should he use it, what results can he expect? How can he realize this basic human dream to find his roots in nature?

This is the job that <u>Lawn Care</u> set for itself, back in 1928. As I look at the other areas we've become involved in since then. . . helping people grow flowers, vegetables, foliage plants, shrubs (and yes, helping golf course superintendents and other turf managers to grow better grass so we can refresh ourselves in recreation). . . I see the evolution of a company that in the midst of change has remained true to its fundamentals. Now we have STI and PTI[1], handbooks and manuals, informative advertising, selling aids, and other customer publications. Our salespeople would be the first to tell you that that's what makes them so powerful; that's what has built the customer base that supports us now.

We'll certainly be faced with critical turning points again during the next half-century, but as our evolution continues, as our product mix shifts to meet new needs and our services change accordingly, the axis that Scotts moves on can't change if we're to maintain our momentum: we must always make it a vital part of our business to keep explaining to our customers what we can do for them. The spirit that conceived of <u>Lawn Care</u>, brought it to life, and committed the energy and resources to make it flourish, is what I consider to be the extraordinary and fundamental spirit of Scotts.

Where are we coming from?

If people are going to devote their energy — and often a major part of their lives — to a company, they should know not just where it is going but where it has been.

Every organization has a past. Ours began when a Civil War veteran, O.M. Scott, returned home to Ohio and decided to "wage peace" by providing clean seed to farmers in the area.

Whether your own company is a hundred-year-old industry icon or a start-up that opened its doors two weeks ago, people are curious about its roots. Why was it founded? What obstacles did it surmount to get where it is now?

This information, conveyed in a CEO's letters, can be a source of pride and inspiration. In fact, that's what we said in a brief note when some Associates asked why we had started this program. By taking advantage of similar opportunities to respond to feedback, you can help people feel listened to and respected.

...sharing some thoughts!

This is the third edition of "Sharing Some Thoughts." Some associates have asked what prompted me to start these communications, and I'd like to take a moment to respond through this note.

Most of you are no doubt aware of the widely acclaimed documentary "Roots," which was shown on television a month or so ago. This series put many of us in touch with a part of the past we had known little about; by showing us what we were, it gave many Americans a resolve and a confidence about what we would become.

Scotts too, has its roots. There are very few companies that have been in existence over a hundred years. There are even fewer with a heritage of leadership that has weathered the trauma of change, and yet remained strong and contemporary.

Although this series of messages was planned weeks before "Roots" reached the TV screen, they share a similar aim. I honestly believe that the more we know about who we really are, the better we can plan what we want to be. Roots are an important part of growing, and I think they are an important part of Scotts.

"Heritage"

One way to help people understand where a company is coming from is to review what its past leaders contributed to its character.

Scotts was an unusual company. Since its founding in 1865, it had had only four previous leaders, and two of them were still alive. Many of us knew one or both of these men personally. The challenge was to accurately describe their contribution to the company, while at the same time showing how they helped develop and reinforce the guiding principles that characterized it.

Researching your own organization's most significant decisions can give you a sense of the attitudes and priorities held by the leader at that time. Combine these snapshots, and you may see a touching picture emerge as it does here in "Heritage."

 Heritage

It's impossible to talk about the roots of Scotts without thinking of the four leaders who shaped its first century. That in itself, when you stop to think about it, is a remarkable circumstance: just four leaders in one hundred years. All four were strong, independent individuals with substantially different personalities, styles and talents. Yet they managed to bring a consistency of purpose to Scotts.

O.M. Scott himself, pioneering weed-free seed for farmers back in 1865, established the strengths that are at the heart of this business when he decided that our growth was to be based on a very fundamental principle: providing value to the customer. It was O.M. who made it part of our business to supply help and information along with a quality product, and to stand behind a guarantee of customer satisfaction.

I think this was a very shrewd but tough decision at that time. With all the turmoil following the end of the Civil War, there were a lot of businessmen out for a fast dollar. Those were the days before seed laws, of course, and many farmers were being victimized by buying cheap, weed-laden seed. O.M. put this company in business for the long haul with his belief that customers will pay for value, and will come back to you if you provide that value consistently.

Dwight Scott, who with his brother Hubert was one of the two "Sons" of the company name, supported that principle 100% when he took over from O.M. Scott. Scotts became the quality front-runner in supplying clean seed to farmers, and Dwight believed in communicating it. (As Chid Mills recalls, "Dwight believed in surrounding the promotion with high-quality everything – our stationery was Swan Linen, an all-rag content paper – we used better shipping bags than anyone else – and the literature was top-grade from the beginning.")

Dwight had an enterprising instinct that soon took us out of farm seed into areas with greater potential: he explored the early-1920s golf course boom by sending his young assistant over to Europe to corner the market in German bentgrass, with such success that by 1928 one out of every five golf courses in this country was using weed-free Scotts seed. Perhaps most significantly for our second 50 years, he recognized the growing potential of home lawns, and began to develop the unique products and services that would help us fulfill the homeowner's demand for quality, weed-free grass.

During this period, there was a happy marriage between Dwight's foresight and the communications ingenuity of the man who became Scotts' third leader, C.B. "Chid" Mills. In 1910 he started working with Dwight as a 14-year-old mail sorter at 10¢ an hour. (As a matter of fact, he was the "young assistant" who came back from Europe with five tons of bentgrass seed.) He became a pioneer in direct-mail advertising, and built a mailing list of lawnowners that still lets us communicate directly with our best customers and prospects. In 1928, he and Dwight created an outstanding vehicle for the "help and information" that they agreed should remain a key part of Scotts – <u>Lawn Care</u>, still going strong after nearly 50 years.

Chid, though retired, is still very much a part of Scotts, and if you have had the good fortune to meet him you can understand immediately why his very personal, down-to-earth way of communicating has been such an important part of our success. Under his guidance, our principles began to express themselves in words a customer could appreciate and rely on. Scotts' commitment to value became a promise, an emotional contract with a customer.

It was P.C. Williams, another Scotts veteran from the late 1920s on, who took this value commitment a step further and built it into something of national scope and size. As Scotts' fourth leader, Paul Williams understood that it was our ability to communicate what we could do for our customer that created our success; that in order to grow we had to understand what the customer's needs were and communicate our solutions in ways that he could comprehend. This is what I define as marketing, and this is an area we were able to capitalize on under Paul's guidance. He took the emotional, direct promise of value and translated it into mass communications, without compromising any of the principles Scotts stands for – an achievement O.M. would be proud of.

I believe we've been very fortunate in these hundred years. Most companies have new leaders who want to leave their own stamp on the business, and generally do this with a shift in direction to some new goals or values. At Scotts, we've had a rare kind of leadership – four men who furthered their company's progress by using their individual strengths and abilities to continue and enlarge upon the efforts of their predecessors.

There's a tough-mindedness that shows through in each of these four leaders, which I feel is worth a few minutes' thought. If you've worked with Paul Williams, I don't think you'll argue about his determination and strong opinions. But Chid Mills, and Dwight Scott, and O.M. weren't any less tough as leaders, in spite of their different personalities. That toughness was what gave them their uncompromising attitude toward the heart of our business – providing value to the customer, and communicating that value – no matter what lures there were toward easier but shorter-ranged gains.

Very few companies can look on that kind of commitment as their heritage, and it's something in which we can all feel a great deal of pride. But we also have to look on it, I think, as something to live up to.

"Chid Mills Remembers"

All of Scotts' former leaders contributed substantially to its character. Paul Williams, my immediate predecessor, was ill, but C.B. "Chid" Mills, who headed Scotts before him, still had a lively interest in the company and a strong emotional attachment to it. I asked Chid to write a message to our people about his memories and feelings for Scotts.

Coming after the foundation had been laid with "Heritage," this moving tribute to the company's spirit had meaning even for newcomers who did not know Chid. As a matter of fact, this was one of the first letters to be inspired by conversations after our half-dozen initial topics had been covered.

 ## …sharing some thoughts!

It seems appropriate in this year of the 50th Anniversary of <u>Lawn Care</u> to invite the originator and first editor of this publication to "share some thoughts" with us. C.B. "Chid" Mills was Scott's Chairman from 1957 to 1967 and President from 1948 to 1956. He gave the company fifty years of service – a feat that probably can not be duplicated in the future.Scotts, Marysville, and Chid Mills are almost synonymous. There are few Scott Associates who have not been directly or indirectly touched by Chid's refreshing sense of humor and his continuing interest in Scotts and its associates. He remains a remarkably young man with a keen interest in the future.

 ## A Letter from Chid Mills

Dear Scott Associate:

It must have been in early spring of the year 1910 when I was walking home from the East Building about 3:15. It must have been my freshman year, as a matter of fact, because I was 14, weighed about 85 pounds and consisted mostly of bones, slightly reddish hair and freckles galore. The seed company was not many years old. In fact, I probably walked past it many times to and from school… although I often went down Fifth Street if by chance I had an extra dime or nickel to spend for peanuts.

How Dwight happened to be standing in the seed company door at the time I'll never know, because he wasn't one to be standing still at any time. "How would you like to come in and help fold the mail?" he asked.

That was how my 50 years as an active Scott Associate began – with that innocent question. How far Scotts has come since then!

I well remember the days when, if you mentioned "Marysville," people thought only of the Women's Reformatory; when the name "Scotts" meant the Scott Paper Company. We vowed to make Scotts Seed first, and we worked hard to get it there – through good years when everything seemed to be going our way, and the lean times when there was not much that stood between us and our outstanding bank loans but determination. True grit was one of the prerequisites for being an Associate then. And it worked. People now know our company's name from coast to coast, and it means much to me to have had some small part in putting Scotts on the map.

But regardless of my interest in the past, the early days when mice were more prevalent than dollars, my chief concern is for the present and future. I have no intention of reminding you about the wonders of the past, the early struggles and the endless working hours. We are now in a new age and I like it. That is where I want to be.

What I miss now is knowing personally all of you. I remember when I could call everyone by name. No more. But as long as you are on the Scott Team, we are teammates. I know you're doing your level best to keep Scotts at the head of the procession. And if you will accept a tribute from a fellow Associate who has racked up enough birthdays in this business to be able to unapologetically say it: I'm proud of you... of your spirit, and of your continuing accomplishments. You are the kind of team Dwight Scott, that man of imagination, would have delighted in.

I wish you all a Very Happy 1978... and I hope that by the start of next year, I'll know all of you better. Meantime, my very warmest regards and May God Bless all of you and your families during the year ahead.

Sincerely,
C.B. "Chid" Mills

"The Pioneers"

Scotts had a history of "firsts" in many areas. As our competition began to catch up with us, there was a feeling in some quarters that our future depended on introducing the next new product quicker than anyone else.

Not only did this place all the burden unfairly on the Research Division, but it just wasn't true of who we were. "The Pioneers" was the letter that resulted.

What do your own people think about what makes your company competitive? Do their perceptions accurately reflect "who we are"?

 ## The Pioneers

We at Scotts have a history of pioneering that goes back to day one, when O.M. Scott decided to market the first truly weed-free seed. Since then, it's been one innovation after another: the first turf fertilizer, the first accurate lawn spreader, the first weed-and–feed. And, since then, a series of technological developments has led us to our high-density fertilizers, our labor-saving control products, and our improved turfgrasses.

It seems as though all we have to do to stay at the forefront of our business is to continue to innovate. All we have to do is make sure our Research Division keeps burning the candle at both ends to give us an unending stream of new products.

With all respect to the great abilities and dedication of our Research people, I have to say I just don't believe that.

As important as new product development is, it won't make or break us as a company all by itself. What our future really depends on is our power to understand and communicate what we can do for people. New technology is just a way to keep expanding that capability.

This does not diminish the heavy responsibility we place on research. Rather, it increases the responsibility of the rest of us to communicate the value of what Research has developed. Not just the "what" but also the "how" – and, most importantly, the "why" (in terms of benefits for the customer).

In an indirect way, this comes back to understanding what business we're in. We are really pioneers of new ideas... and before we can sell a new product, we usually have to sell the new idea that it's based on. That makes the job much tougher, of course – you can't just put a new idea in a box and say "Special Introductory Offer" and expect people to snap it up like hotcakes. You have to understand it. And you have to make other people understand it.

This is the responsibility I mentioned earlier. It starts with us – with all of us, not just our R&D people. In fact, we are all R&D people when it comes to our future. "Research," after all, means "investigating thoroughly" and "development" means "opening" or "revealing." And that's the business not just of a couple of hundred people who work with test tubes and turf plots, nor just the handful of Marketing associates who work directly on communications, but of all of us at Scotts. Each of us needs to understand thoroughly what our business is, and what the ideas are that we are trying to reveal. Each of us, even if indirectly, contributes to or supports the overall communication effort. Each of us has the choice of either "standing pat" in what we're doing or, by always looking for an improved method here and a new wrinkle there, of being a "pioneer."

That's our future. And that's our challenge!

How We Do Business

Why do our customers value us?

For many consumer goods companies, successful selling is a simple matter of exchanging products for dollars. For Scotts, the personal involvement of the purchaser was also an essential part of the process. A bag of Turf Builder can't produce a great-looking lawn by itself; someone needs to put time and care into applying it.

Personal involvement turned our consumers into partners who had a stake in our products' success. Looking at an improved lawn, they could feel justifiable pride in their efforts, and the wisdom of their choice of Scotts was reinforced.

This, again, underlined the importance of trust. Few people are willing to devote their time and energy to a task that might not be worth it. Scotts product users had to be confident that their personal involvement would pay off with good results. Consequently, we needed to provide useful information — "what" and "why" as well as "how" and "when" — that would encourage and empower them.

In the final analysis, the outcome that both we and our customers sought was the result of an equation with three factors: their personal involvement, shared information that helped them use the product at the proper time in the proper way, and last, the quality of the product itself. Our marketing skill and success involved all these ingredients. In the letters that follow, we suggested to Scott Associates that when looking at new opportunities, it was important to remember that these were our strengths.

In considering this topic yourself, it's useful to ask what is unique about the way your company does business. To get beyond the clichés of "we have quality people" or "we are customer-driven," you may want to talk to your customers (including intermediaries as well as end users), along with people in the everyday workforce.

"Trust"

Market research told us Scotts was unusual in that consumers were loyal to our company, not to our brand or our products. These days, it's still true that people tend to trust a brand (such as Craftsman) or a product (such as Tide) without necessarily having strong feelings of trust about the company behind them.

Among the exceptions, Hallmark comes close to what we tried to do at Scotts. Their theme, "When you care enough to send the very best," is supported by the highest-quality advertising. I never have to think twice about letting my grandchildren watch a "Hallmark Hall of Fame" presentation on TV. Another example is L.L. Bean, the outdoor gear and apparel company, which commands a high degree of customer loyalty. It is interesting to note that they, like Scotts, have a longstanding "satisfaction guaranteed" policy.

Do your customers trust your company, your brand, or your product? You might consider discussing this topic in a letter like the one on the next pages.

 Trust

"It's a company you can trust."

"Well, they have integrity."

"Everybody I know has always had luck with Scotts products; it's a reputable company."

Time and time again, as we ask consumers what they think about Scotts products without revealing our own identity as the questioners, we hear answers like these... answers which reveal a consumer trust that most companies would give their eyeteeth to possess.

Our business, as these comments suggest, is more than just a transaction in which the consumer exchanges dollars for our product. It's a business in which there are really three elements combining to make that sale:

First, the personal involvement of the purchaser. We don't offer him instant results with a snap of the fingers; we require him to share part of the effort, so that he'll be part of the success. Whether he calls it "luck" or good judgment, his success becomes a personal achievement. And that, I believe, helps bring him back to Scotts.

Second, the information and knowledge we share with the consumer. This is an important part of what we provide to help guarantee success. Without it, the best-intentioned consumer and the most carefully researched product could just be a recipe for disaster.

Third, of course, is the quality of the product itself. At times we're tempted, as every company is, to lower our quality standards by whatever degree is necessary in order to hold the line on consumer prices. Would consumers notice it if we did reduce quality? Eventually – but inevitably – yes, they would. And while they might or might not still trust the product, inevitably they would trust Scotts less.

As the consumer quotes above indicate, our market research reveals that Scotts is relatively unique in the consumer goods industry, in that consumers trust us as a company. Generally speaking, it's far more common for consumers to trust a product than its manufacturer.

Trust is generated by the three elements I mentioned earlier – personal involvement of the purchaser, a sharing of knowledge, and a quality product – bonded together by our two-way relationship with the consumer. We ask him to share his experiences with us, we try to solve his problems, and if all else fails, he knows he can come to us and we'll stand behind our products with a refund. We are involved with him, as he is involved with us.

Our marketing success thus far involves all these elements; as we look at new opportunities, we must remember that these are our strengths. If we try to go in a direction that doesn't utilize them, we're in a foreign land where we can't derive any benefit from the strengths and skills we have developed.

It's hard to put a price tag on the value of consumer trust to today's and tomorrow's business. It's a priceless ingredient, worth more to us than anything we could buy. Once we begin to take away from it... once we begin to lose the consumer's trust by skimping on the quality of our response to him... we risk losing the greatest part of our success.

Trust can't be bought. It can only be built, bit by bit, by all of us.

"Involvement"

Lawn care services were a topic of great debate among our management staff. Some were convinced that these services could eventually put Scotts out of business, and that we would have to go into lawn care ourselves in order to survive.

However, the consumer's personal involvement, and sharing information that helped him get good results, were two of the three legs on which our company had built its success. If we became a lawn service company, product quality would remain the only leg for us to stand on.

Thus, a move in that direction required careful thought. We would need to identify how to replace those two missing legs in order to retain Scotts' reputation and our consumers' loyalty. This issue is addressed indirectly in "Involvement."

As you consider your own business, are there aspects of its success that are unique? When you have an opportunity to do something radically different, what qualities of the way you do business are worth protecting?

 Involvement

There is a tremendous emphasis in society today on convenience. Many of us buy "convenience foods," shop in conveniently located multi-store shopping centers, and even arrange our working hours, with flextime, to suit our convenience.

Products that promise greater convenience are hard to quarrel with, because they seem to solve a problem: the finite limitations of time. If consumers can achieve their desired result and spend fewer hours in the effort, none of us would deny them that benefit – in fact, we'd probably be next in line ourselves to buy the product.

You can see how the logical extension of that thought, for a shrewd marketer, is to try to totally <u>eliminate</u> the consumer's time-investment in the effort. But here is where some companies run into trouble.

You may remember that a few years ago one of the major multifood corporations brought out a revolutionary new cake mix. It was almost totally self-contained: no longer did the consumer have to add eggs or milk or anything else – just water. By cutting down on the <u>involvement</u> required of the user, the company was able to promise great convenience in preparation time.

The product was a terrible bomb. Consumers didn't want that much of the preparation done for them. The result just wasn't "their" cake, because they hadn't been allowed to contribute enough to its creation. The company, recognizing its mistake, backed up a few steps and changed its formulations to allow consumers to mix in the eggs and milk again.

In some businesses, there is just no substitute for the <u>personal involvement</u> of the consumer. Ours is such a business.

As hard as we may work to make our products more convenient – through innovations which decrease weight and bulk, increase ease of handling, and minimize the time required to see results – we should never forget that if we totally eliminate the consumer's involvement, we eliminate much of the pride and pleasure that comes from being surrounded by green and growing things.

The consumer is a variable – and is well aware of that fact. He or she might buy the same Scotts product in the same store on the same day that a neighbor does, and the two of them could have totally different results. They've been required to make a series of decisions, and to put in some personal effort, which are vitally important to their success with the product. When the results are good, they share the credit, almost as if they were partners with Scotts.

I believe that this process of involvement is what ties the knot between the consumer and Scotts; it's an important link that should be part of everything Scotts does.

It's almost as though we were selling products with a missing piece. Because we've always recognized that the consumer isn't buying a "what," but a "how-to": how to have a thick, healthy lawn; how to have a successful vegetable garden; how to grow beautiful and vigorous ornamentals. We offer our products and information to consumers with the understanding that they are the missing piece... crucial to our success, just as we're important to theirs. That's the true definition of a partnership, and I believe they perceive it as one.

The alternative is to present them with a completed result. That is the job of a supplier, not a partner; and while it may produce satisfaction, I doubt whether it produces the degree of pride, pleasure, and loyalty that comes from involving them in the process.

Convenience, as the Latinists among you have known all along, is really the key to our success: it literally means coming together. As we keep working to make "growing things" more convenient for our customers, let's not forget that we want them to know we're working together. It's called "involvement."

"Phantom Products"

A phantom product, as mentioned earlier, is one whose value can't be judged at point of sale, or sometimes even at point of use. In many cases, our society tries to resolve this problem with regulation. From multivitamins to mutual funds, we are encouraged to look at lists of numbers and try to deduce which choice will perform best, which offers the most value, which one to trust.

But trust between a company and its customers can't be legislated. It originates when customers understand that the company trusts them and tries to help them get what they want. That is the key to success with any type of product or service — but especially with phantom products.

 ## Phantom Products

Normally, when you go into a store to make a purchase – whether it's a lawnmower, a spreader, a garden rake or something else – you can use information about the product to prove its claims of durability, ease of use, maneuverability or handiness to your satisfaction, before you spend a dime on it. If nothing else, you can base a decision – right or wrong – on an eyeball assessment of whether it "looks like good quality."

What does Scotts offer the consumer at point of purchase? A bag or box, filled with little pieces of chemical formula or seed. You just can't "prove" the merit of a product like this before you buy it – it's an unknown, a phantom.

At the next stage – usage – some other products which were phantoms at the point of purchase became "real." As soon as you open a can of paint, for instance, and begin painting your house, you can prove to yourself whether the product claims of the right color, even spreading, odorlessness, or one-coat coverage are really true. Some claims, like "long-lasting," may need more time to evaluate, but by and large you know at that point whether the product works or not.

What does Scotts offer during usage? An opportunity to see the pieces of formula or seed fall out a spreader onto your lawn or garden. Still hard to see any proof of performance or quality.

Finally, our products require people to wait several weeks for results. Meantime, a lot of things may happen to affect those results: application errors, too much rain, too much sun, too much cold, and so forth. During all this time, our customers have absolutely no reason to trust the product to perform as it's supposed to. But they've bought it and applied it, in the confidence that the performance will be there. Not only that, but they continue to buy more Scott products that most of our competitors' combined.

Why?

They trust <u>Scotts</u>.

It's as simple as that. Consumers depend on what we've promised <u>as a company</u> – and their trust is in us as a company, not in any individual product per se. We strengthen that contract by offering a guarantee, not of product performance, but of personal satisfaction. In effect, Scotts' promise bridges the gap between the product itself, and the results the buyer anticipates.

Manufacturers can be required by law to provide product information, but all the facts and figures in the world can't satisfy a skeptical consumer faced with a phantom product. What we do at Scotts is based on a much more sensitive and fundamental law: caring enough about our customers' opinion that we try to earn their loyalty and trust in every way we can.

Given the nature of our products, this broader responsibility is essential for our success. And, in the truest sense of the word, it is real consumerism.

"The Value of Excellence"
"Price and the Customer"

Quality is made up of little things, but it's the biggest thing. As hard as a company may struggle to fully serve its customers, there is always the temptation to take shortcuts. At Scotts, the relative expense of high quality always found its way into budget discussions. If we lowered our manufacturing quality or cut back on our communications programs, couldn't we offer our products at a lower price?

We addressed this issue in a message called "Price and the Customer," concluding that the customer is really the only one who can tell us if we are on the right track. Lo and behold, a Scotts consumer in Florissant, Missouri, later wrote to our Customer Service Manager, Fred Sweet, about that very subject. I forwarded this letter to our Associates with a short cover note that ended, "Be sure to read the last paragraph, just above his signature. <u>There</u> is the value of excellence."

When you read this unsolicited letter (which I've called "The Value of Excellence") followed by our "Price and the Customer" message, it's more than interesting. To me, it's very inspiring.

 "The Value of Excellence"

Dear Mr. Sweet,

I received your questionnaire and copy of "Success With Annual Flowers" in the mail today. Accompanying this letter is the completed questionnaire, and I'd like to take this opportunity to tell you about the success I've had with the excellent products manufactured by O.M. Scott.

We have owned our present home for two years. The lawn was more dirt and weeds than grass that first spring. I decided to give Scotts products a try on the recommendation of my brother-in-law. It seemed easier than starting all over.

The results to date have been little short of phenomenal. I now have grass where I thought even weeds could not survive. The first several applications were done with Turf Builder Plus Two. The dandelions disappeared in just a few days. Astonishing! This past spring I counted four dandelions in the entire front lawn. The grass is now thicker, greener and healthier than I would ever have thought possible. The last two applications in the fall were done with Turf Builder alone. I am eagerly awaiting spring to see what improvements the lawn will show this year.

Am I sold on Scotts' products? I wouldn't use anything but Scotts. My father allowed me to treat his lawn last year after seeing the results I achieved. He noticed a difference in his lawn within a month. Most notably, he had to cut it more often. I don't know if he appreciates that, but the grass is now thicker and greener.

Not only does Scotts offer the finest lawn care products on the market, but you show a genuine concern for the people who buy your products. I know of no other company which offers the money back guarantee Scotts does. The toll free number to call with lawn problems, the offer to evaluate any lawn samples sent to your offices, the Lawn Care magazine and the network of Lawn Care Professionals are all unique to the industry. Scotts is a customer service company. The interest in the customer goes beyond selling him a bag of fertilizer. That is a most refreshing attitude to encounter in this day.

I look forward to receiving your recommendations by return mail. Just tell me what product(s) to put in my Scotts Spreader this spring and summer to achieve the results indicated on the questionnaire.

If anyone at Scotts has ever wondered if the extra efforts Scotts' people put forth are worth it, tell them yes. I'm a customer for life – because Scotts cares.

Sincerely,
(Name removed for privacy)

P.S. Just a closing note about the local lawn care professional. He's the owner of Handy Man Hardware here in Florissant. He answered my questions when no one else could or would. Next time Scotts' representative is through this area, tell him to pat the "pro" on the back. He knows his stuff.

 ## Price and the Customer

Outsiders and newcomers to our business invariably ask, "Why is Scotts high-priced? Can't you produce products at lower costs?"

Obviously we could. We could use lower-grade ingredients. We could scrimp on research, cut down our testing, limit our new product development. We could scrap our Polyform and Trionized plants and manufacture our fertilizers by simple and inexpensive mechanical mixing, like just about everybody else. We could put our products in plain brown bags. We could even stop telling people about the benefits and results those products offer, by eliminating our educational, advertising and sales support.

But if we took any of those steps, would our value – the cost per unit of benefit – be maintained? Not likely. We would have lost the very essence of what has kept Scotts standing out in the marketplace. Sure, we might enjoy a temporary sales bonanza with a cheaper product. Our reputation ensures that. But what about later on, as we become just another face in the crowd? What happens when people start saying, "Ho hum, there's no difference in value between Scotts and anybody else, so I'll just buy whatever's on sale at the lowest price"?

On the other hand, I'm not so naïve as to believe that a product – regardless of how good it is – can be sold at any price. In a competitive environment, manufacturers have to continually work on balancing the cost of a product's benefits against the lowest possible price they can charge, and still make enough money to keep the business growing. Scotts is no different: We are constantly reevaluating our products' benefits, including all supporting factors. Do they justify what they add to the price of the product? Can they be reduced without significantly impairing end results? Is there a way to provide them more economically?

Of course, in the final analysis it's the customer who really determines whether or not the price/value relationship of a product is valid. They have complete freedom of choice, and either they buy or they don't buy. More importantly, they either keep on buying, or they switch to something else.

In our case, our leading share-of-market for so many years is powerful evidence that our commitment to high-quality, high-benefit products supported by helpful communications is regarded as good "value" by our customers. It's a commitment we've had for over one hundred years. It just comes down to giving the customer what he really wants, and what he can't get as well from any other source – regardless of the cost.

And that, I think, is the strength of our position. We know our capability; we know what customers want; and we know what they have come to expect from Scotts. If we continue to do our job right, <u>value</u>, rather than price, will keep our customers trusting us and coming back again and again. And that's what will keep us growing.

How do we succeed?

There are no commodity businesses. There are only businesses with weak consumer relationships.

Scotts had every opportunity to be one of those weak businesses. We sold primarily through intermediaries such as hardware stores, lawn & garden stores, and other retailers. If a store decided to build traffic by deeply discounting Turf Builder, or a clerk advised a consumer against Scott products, what could we do about it?

In reality, we were far from powerless because of the relationships we established directly with consumers through <u>Lawn Care</u>, TV advertising, and so on. These relationships were even stronger because they were two-way. We encouraged consumer phone calls and letters, and always responded personally. In fact, we had a program called Wet Feet in which every senior manager took a turn answering the phones of our Consumer Hotline and dealing with callers' problems, questions, and opinions. The lawnowners who called in probably had no idea that they were speaking with a director of marketing or a vice president of legal affairs, but this program helped all of us keep in touch with consumer needs.

When a company succeeds in communicating value in ways like these, stronger relationships result. A preference based on a perception of value is much harder to overturn than a preference based solely on price. Thus, our focus on communicating Scotts' value directly to the consumer gave us influence over our delivery channel, the retailer.

This was the answer to "How Do We Succeed?" Explaining it in our letter program allowed us to address some criticisms of the way Scotts did business, and explain why this unusual approach was actually an intrinsic part of our success.

How does your business succeed? The answer may not be obvious, requiring you to be clear in your perception and in the way you articulate it to your audience.

"The Little Revolutions"

Just what made our products better than the competition? It was impossible for the average consumer to tell at point of sale, or even at point of use. So why should they pay more for Turf Builder than Brand X?

In this letter, we discussed how Scotts benefited from telling consumers what we could do for them. Our commitment to educating people about growing and maintaining grass was recognized all over the country, and Scotts was respected for giving away this information at no charge.

Open communication has the power to unlock people's loyalty. Once they understand and identify with the purpose of the company and the values it stands for, then — and only then — will they try their best to help it succeed. This is as true outside your business, with consumers, as it is on the inside.

 ## The Little Revolutions

"What our future really depends on is our power to understand and communicate what we can do for people."

I honestly believe that's the key to our success. And as I mentioned in a recent memo, I think it's a responsibility all of us at Scotts share. We're in business to help people achieve their natural desire to surround themselves with green and growing things. For over a hundred years, we've been pioneering new ways to do that. And – some times better than others – we have communicated those new ways so well that people have accepted them with enthusiasm.

Let me give you an example: the marketing of Windsor. A revolutionary grass of its time... ten years in research... a real breakthrough in improved Kentucky bluegrasses. Why did it succeed? <u>Because we told people what it could do for them</u>. We told them about the vigorous rhizoming that meant it was denser and stronger and filled in bare spots quicker. We told them about the care we took in trying to clean everything out of the box except pure Windsor seed, so they wouldn't have weeds growing up along with their new lawns. We didn't just say Windsor was a totally different kind of grass. We told them why.

Good communication, I think, has to start with understanding the small things that open up people's minds. Often that opening-up happens because you're telling them something they never understood before. It's almost as if a little revolution goes on in somebody's mind, each time you share knowledge with him. He may not remember every detail you tell him, but he will never forget that you value him enough to educate him to the point where he can evaluate what you can do for him. That is why we continue to devote much of our collective time and energy on activities such as our toll-free Hotline, personalized answers by mail, Weed-Ident service, seasonal <u>Lawn Care</u> mailings, in-store booklet guides, STI classes, homeowner clinics, and so forth.

There is a terrible risk – let alone a substantial expense – and many companies do not dare or care to get involved. They rely instead on a "me-too" approach, riding the coattails of a more courageous or more foresighted competitor – which means they have given up hopes of leadership. Or they may try to dazzle their customers with the sheer technological brilliance of breakthrough after breakthrough, without explaining why the customer should care. But many companies with great technological resources have gone broke when somebody less brilliant, but with more understanding of what turns people on, took the great idea and explained it better. You may know the old saying: "A new idea belongs to whoever explains it best."

We fully intend to continue pressing for technological breakthroughs, for innovations, for leadership. But our growth, and our future success as pioneers of ideas, depend on how well we can succeed with the "little revolutions"... the sharing of knowledge that can make a customer out of a prospect, and a client out of a customer. Over the next hundred years, our course will be charted not so much by whether we are first to create something, but whether we are first to make people understand what it can do for them. ▮

"Thinking Cheap"

The word "cheap" is a scary word to many companies, who fear people will think it means their products are low-quality. However, Scotts was so often accused of being high-priced by critics (including some within our own ranks) that we chose this term to shock people into a different way of thinking.

Interestingly, when this letter was written, value had not become the buzzword that it is today. But it was a crucial concept in helping us explain how a relatively expensive product could really be a great buy.

 Thinking Cheap

One of the most interesting things about Scotts to me is that people think we are expensive. I say "interesting," but you can probably guess that I also mean "frustrating." You see, when it comes to the cost of our products, I have a bias.

My bias is that I think our products are cheap.

Is that really true? Let me explore it a little with you.

We are a nation of jumpers-to-conclusions, when it comes to things with which we're unfamiliar. If you don't know much about fertilizers and you're in a store looking at them for the first time, unless someone tells you different you might jump to the conclusion that all fertilizers are alike, and you'd pick the one that cost least. You might eventually regret that decision. But again, you might not, if nobody tells you what another product could have done for you.

The fact of the matter is, price is a very unreliable thing to base a buying decision on. All it really tells you is how much the manufacturer put into the products, and how much the retailer values it. (Or how little.)

Price doesn't tell you how long the product will last, how much trouble it will give you in the meantime, or whether you will have any occasion to be glad you bought it. And that's what you really want to know before you buy, isn't it?

If some genius could invent a cost-per-unit-of-benefit standard with which we could reprice every turf product on the market, you know who'd come out ahead, hands down?

That's what I mean, I think our products are cheap.

There's already a general word for that cost-per-unit-of-benefit measure: VALUE. They haven't found a way yet to standardize it so you can mark a value rating on a bag or box, which means it's up to us to get the story across to the conclusion-jumpers. This isn't just something that'd be nice to do so people will smile when they see the Scotts name – it's something we <u>must</u> do to survive.

When someone is comparing a Scotts product, pound for pound, with a lower-priced product, if we don't tell him something about the added units of benefit we give him, why in the world should we expect him to spend more money with us? If he's a homeowner, he's paying out his own hard-earned cash; if he's a turf superintendent, he's giving us money he could use to hire another worker or to buy a new piece of equipment.

There is no other way to sell value than by education. As I mentioned in an earlier memo, it is only this sharing of knowledge that gives a customer a basis to evaluate what we can do for him... and what our competitors can't do.

A Scotts customer has to understand the relationship between price and value. He has to understand that "cheap" seed that's full of chaff and weeds, that doesn't produce good coverage or healthy turf and costs a minor fortune later in herbicides and overseeding, is pretty expensive in the long run – which makes it outrageously expensive on the value scale. "Cheap" fertilizer that doesn't produce any response, or burns the turf when you accidentally overlap, or peters out after stimulating the grass to grow so fast you end up mowing twice as often, can be much more expensive than its original purchase price in frustration, time, and the cost of corrective measures.

My grandfather used to tell me, "Poor people always buy the cheapest shoes. That's why they're always poor." If all you think about is price, that may get you out the door and down the block in your new shoes. But ten thousand steps later, value is what you notice. How much will you <u>really</u> have paid per unit of benefit over the life of those shoes?

I called this memo "Thinking Cheap," and you might suspect I'm saying "don't do it." But I'm not really. Everybody's got to think cheap; nobody's got money to waste. What I'm saying is that we've got to communicate what "cheap" really means: the best value, the greatest real savings. If we can get a customer to really think cheap, we will have him thinking Scotts.

"Who Is the Real Boss?"

In contrast to many businesses that sell directly to their end user, Scotts had a two-step marketing process: our *customer* was the retailer, who in turn displayed and sold our products to the *consumer*. Although many of our people's jobs were governed by dealing with retailer problems and demands, it was vital to remember that our ultimate bond needed to be with the consumer.

I don't want to slight or disparage the many retailers who became our business partners in distributing Scotts products. After all, I came to Scotts from a retail background myself. But valuable though these intermediaries' contribution was, they were only a vehicle to reach the ultimate user. With a strong enough consumer franchise, a company like Scotts could survive the loss of a customer. (Ironically, the strength of that franchise more often than not influenced retail chains to keep doing business with us.)

As the rise of Internet marketing has demonstrated, a "customer" may well change over time. But when your business is based on satisfying a basic human need, as Scotts' is, your consumer will not change.

 ## Who Is the Real Boss?
Who do you work for?

If you stood at the door of any of our offices or plants and asked this question of every Scott associate who passed you, I imagine you'd end up with a clipboard full of answers in no time. "I work for John Jones." "I work for Mary Smith." "I work for a division of Scotts." You might even get a fiercely independent "I work for myself!"

Every one of these responses would be true, and yet they're only part of the answer. Because when it comes right down to it, we all work for the same person – OUR BOSS, THE CONSUMER.

"Sure," you may say, "that's nothing new. I knew that all along." And I agree, you may have known this basic principle for years. However, those of you who have been out on the front lines, so to speak, may have had more opportunity to see how important the consumer really is to our success.

The consumer combines the best elements of a good boss with the worst elements of a bad one. If we do a good job for him, he'll sing our praises to everyone within earshot, which is the kind of acceptance that can mean significantly greater rewards for us. On the other hand, if he thinks we're putting something over on him, or fail to measure up to his expectations, he'll be equally outspoken to all his friends and neighbors about our failings, with the result that everyone in the neighborhood will eventually hear that we betrayed his trust. This can easily shatter the crucial (but often fragile) confidence all those other people were building up in us... and next time those "bosses" are about to make a purchase, they'll look someplace else.

Our business depends 100% on whether we establish, sustain, and strengthen our consumers' confidence in us. That's why, as you probably know, we place such tremendous importance on consumer communications like <u>Lawn Care</u> – which now reaches close to two million households – STI, PTI, and the Consumer Hot Line.

Each associate is a big part of our success in this endeavor. Whether full-time or not – you're a representative of Scotts to the consumer. You may have a dozen or a hundred chances to affect a consumer's decision about Scotts in the course of a year, even if it's only in the way you answer a telephone inquiry, or in what you say to help out a confused neighbor at the local store's lawn and garden department. In those cases you have a real opportunity by making your boss, the consumer, feel that he made a smart decision in turning to Scotts.

It's hard to go far wrong if we keep our boss's interests at heart. We know the consumer wants our help in achieving green, pleasant surroundings for himself; and if we can do that job well, we should profit from it, as individuals and as a company. In the process, we have essential tasks to perform – controlling costs, meeting forecasts, manufacturing quality products, and so on – but in the final analysis it's still the consumer who'll evaluate how well we're doing at the job he pays us to do. He's the person we've got to please. So in order to keep improving, we need to look at that job not just through our own eyes, but also through the consumer's eyes… not as an end in itself, but as a means to an end.

There's nothing new about this concept of the consumer. In fact, it's really just a matter of getting back to our roots, to the days when everybody in the company – from O.M. Scott on down – dealt with consumers and learned firsthand what they wanted. We've redefined our markets since then and will be making further definitions as time goes on… but even in the retail products market, where we have a two step distribution process, we must recognize that it's the consumer who keeps us in business. As important as he is to us, the retailer himself is only a vehicle to reach the consumer. We can't afford to lose our direct contact with the user, no matter how much we grow. In fact, I'd go so far as to say that if this company ever goes out of business, it will be because we have fallen out of touch with the consumer.

Try to see your job through the consumer's eyes. Remind yourself of what he really wants, and ask yourself how you could best meet his need. Then you may end up with the kind of recognition that three outstanding Scott associates obtained in the attached letter from one of our bosses.

He sounds like a man who's happy with our work.

To the President
O.M. Scott & Sons
Marysville, Ohio

Dear Sir,

I'm writing to you because I feel certain that you will be interested in my recent experience with your company. In these times when we have come to expect a lack of interest in our problems, I would like to tell the rest of the world – so feel free to pass this on to your Editor of Lawn Care if you so desire. But "your people" have been so outstandingly kind and considerate to me that I wanted you to know.

I have – and dearly love – a Scotts Electric mower which I purchased in 1963. When the motor quit in mid-summer, I tried unsuccessfully to have it repaired here in Indianapolis and was told that the motor was a complex, custom-made – and extremely difficult to repair. So, in desperation, I called your "hot-line" and a well-informed man told me that the mower had not been made since 1962 and that very few parts were still available – but he gave me the name of Mr. Simpson to call in your "Mechanical Service" section, as an authority on what is still available. And authority he was – and sent me one of the last replacement motors – and at a price which had to be from the 1962 list! And sent on open account by UPS the same day I called. So that would have made an impressive story if it had stopped there, but that was the easy part.

A few weeks later I had installed the motor but had nearly destroyed the flange that holds the blade, so could only operate with difficulty. So... another call to Mr. Simpson who had no spare flanges, but whose Supervisor offered to have your machine shop make the part for me – for $5.00!

I was overwhelmed, but accepted and received within a week the new part. So my fifteen year old mower is once again purring happily and I am a dedicated Scotts booster forevermore.

Sorry I've been so wordy, but I thought you'd like to know. To me, this was your typical story of a small-town treatment of a neighbor around the turn of the century. When I tell my friends about it, I'm certain that they think I'm stretching the truth – people just don't do that!

Most sincerely,
(Name removed for privacy)

"Satisfaction Guaranteed"

What consumers bought in a Scotts package wasn't what they really wanted. They wanted a great-looking, healthy lawn. We only provided a means to achieve that desire. When they paid their money, there was absolutely no way for them to know whether they would be happy with the results.

So we gave them a unique No-Quibble Guarantee. This guarantee was not limited to satisfactory performance of the product, as defined by some agronomist or attorney. Instead, the consumer alone determined whether he or she was satisfied with the result. It's like offering a guarantee that you will feel terrific wearing a new outfit. Only you can decide whether or not the product lives up to its promise.

The No-Quibble Guarantee required us to trust the consumer as much as we wanted the consumer to trust us. In my opinion, this was a low-risk proposition. Most people try to live up to the trust of others, not take advantage of it. And in fact, we found that very few people asked for their money back.

 Satisfaction Guaranteed

I've heard it said that nothing baffles man as much as straight talk and plain dealing. When it comes to something unfamiliar, we are all as suspicious as a pack of sea lawyers, trying to X-ray every angle to figure out what the "catch" is.

In the case of Scotts, I'd modify that original comment to say that few things seem to baffle man as much as the "No-Quibble Guarantee." Yet of all the thousands of words we generate each year in explaining about ourselves and our products, I believe the two sentences of this guarantee tell our customers more about Scotts than nearly anything else we can say.

> "If for any reason you are not satisfied with results after using this product, you are entitled to your money back. Simply send us evidence of purchase and we will mail you a refund check promptly."

A very plain and simple statement, wouldn't you agree? It doesn't leave much room for misinterpretation or legal hairsplitting – what it means is "if this product doesn't do what you wanted it to, we'll give you your money back." You'll note that what we're actually guaranteeing is not the product, but the customer's satisfaction. And satisfaction, or course, is purely in the eye of the beholder; there's no way a researcher, or a lawyer, or anybody else can predict in advance how high a customer's satisfaction threshold is.

This approach doesn't baffle our customers; it makes immediate sense to them. But it sure puzzles a lot of other people, especially outsiders to Scotts. They want to know: how can we possibly afford to make that promise; won't we lose our shirts?

We make that promise for two reasons. One, because we believe our products will work, and we want our customers to have confidence in them when they buy. They _have_ to buy on confidence, because we deal essentially in a phantom product. They just can't kick our tires or take us out for a test drive before putting their money down on the counter.

There's another side to that same point. Before we can market a product with this strong a guarantee, we, at Scotts, are forced to make sure we can have a good deal of confidence in it ourselves. This is a horrendous management discipline... we can never afford to rush a product to market half-tested or badly researched, no matter how anxiously we think our customers are waiting for it.

In addition to wanting to communicate our own confidence about our products, we have a second reason for making this promise to our customers: to let them know that we have faith in them. We're being as open with them as a company can be... and I believe that with this guarantee, we make it pretty clear that we basically trust them. What we're saying is in effect "we want you to have a nice lawn; we want it so badly that we're willing to put our faith in you on the line."

People usually fulfill the expectation you have of them, and our customers are very slow to abuse that trust. Our refunds generally run at a very low percent of sales, year after year... and even at that, it's not unheard-of for us to receive a personal check in the mail from one of our refundee customers, with a nice note saying his complaint was premature and his Scotts products are indeed working as they were supposed to.

All in all, I suspect that we run a lower risk in talking about our guarantee than if we kept quiet about it. When we are this straightforward with a customer about our confidence in our products and our faith in his honesty, his first inclination if something goes wrong on his lawn is to wonder whether it wasn't his fault rather than ours. If we hadn't made him aware of our guarantee, he'd have little basis for gauging our reliability and integrity as a manufacturer... and I tend to think he'd be much more inflexible in demanding his money back.

This simple concept of a promise between us and our customers is one of the things about Scotts that outsiders find most difficult to understand. We guarantee something that we have no control over – satisfaction. But we do everything we can to make that satisfaction possible... and because we guarantee it, we end up creating some control over it.

With the "No-Quibble Guarantee," we try to remove as many barriers as possible between us and the customer. In fact, the only condition we place on a customer taking advantage of it is that he send us some proof of purchase – and that's primarily so we know how much money to refund to him. We don't want any customer of ours to suffer a loss as a result of having trusted us; ideally, we'd like to restore things to a point a little on the plus side, so he has some encouragement to try us again.

In the process, we're strengthening a bond of trust and confidence between ourselves and our customers. That, rather than the dollars and cents that are refunded, is the bottom line on our guarantee. And that's what really makes it something of value.

"Change"

Life is an evolutionary process of defining one's principles and trying to do a better job of living by them. For example, when I was 22 years old listening to the old sergeant, I didn't fully grasp what leadership meant. Over the years, its meaning has gained breadth and richness for me. I have learned different ways of implementing this fundamental truth, but the truth itself has stayed the same.

People can change themselves by adopting the qualities that make a good individual — integrity, fairness, and honesty, for example. The same is true of companies. When you know what you believe in, be willing to change to protect your principles. Just don't change your principles.

To an extent, the letter titled "Change" was a response to some people's perception that we were fixated on the status quo. They were genuinely concerned that Scotts might be left in the dust if we weren't alert to new ways of doing business. You may wish to consider a message about this important topic if your company has turned down opportunities to change, or if it has changed a great deal in recent years.

 ## Change

So far these thoughts have attempted to deal with Scotts' heritage of fundamental and enduring values – "principles" might be another word. As a group, they're sort of a North Star of the conscience, something that doesn't change, something we can take our bearings from to make sure we're tracking on course. Not everyone will agree with all of these values, but they're a basic part of Scotts today, and will be an important part of our future.

Does this mean we'll stay exactly as we are for the rest of our existence? I fervently hope not… because if we do, that existence will probably be short and relatively unhappy.

The need and the urgency for change is part of the fabric of every company. Whether we like it or not, everything around us is changing: our customers' habits and attitudes change, the economy changes, the climate changes, we ourselves change as individuals. As a living organism, Scotts must adapt to new conditions to survive, or – like the dinosaurs – we'll be left behind by evolution.

The most crucial part of change, it seems to me, is making sure that none of our fundamental values are lost in the transition. They are the constants that must not vary; if we're considering a shift in course to take advantage of more favorable conditions, it's our values that should tell us how helpful that shift would be in terms of where we really want to go.

It concerns me that there's somewhat of a feeling these days that you have to feed people Pablum about the future, because they will resist or ignore change. And it's true, some of us do see change – any change – as bad. Nobody likes agony, and all change carries with it some agony. But I believe most people will respond to change if they can see the benefit, even if it means some initial difficulty or hardship. People do respond to challenge when it means a real opportunity to grow and to prosper... and our fundamental values can help us determine in advance just how much opportunity we can expect any change to provide.

In fact, sometimes the yardstick of our values is the only way to estimate how much a potential change could benefit us. By and large, we're a young group here at Scotts; most associates haven't worked for many other companies, and don't have a lot of prior experience to draw from in evaluating the potential results of a change. We all have opinions on changes we'd like to see in the company – associate relationship, for instance – but how many of us have worked with a company that didn't give a darn about its employees? Many of us have strong opinions about the competitiveness of our product quality standards and our prices – but how many of us have experienced the frustrating job of selling "me-too" products when you're just another face in the crowd? Oftentimes, it seems, we can only appreciate the good when we've had to struggle through the bad to get there.

Our principles can save us a lot of <u>unnecessary</u> agony, because they remind us what we're in business for: to help fulfill people's need for natural greenery; to provide a superior value; to inform our customers so they can better evaluate our capability; to act as true associates in an enterprise. We've spent over a hundred years exploring and verifying these fundamentals, but essentially they've stayed the same – while Scotts itself has evolved from a family store selling farm seed, to an international company marketing everything from little packages of fertilizer to big broadcast spreaders that weigh nearly a quarter of a ton. That's real change, and there'll be more of it in the future. I have no doubt about that.

The law of change, in fact, is a fundamental value all by itself. If it were written down, it would probably be something like <u>"Change when it's necessary to protect your principles... but don't change your principles</u>."

Sounds easy? You can guess how difficult a process it really is. But it's one which I hope we never stop going through, no matter what the agony – because once that happens, we're adrift.

---

[1]Scotts Training Institute and Professional Turf Institute.

Chapter Eight

The Scotts Letters:
One Man's Opinion

Bringing out the best in each other -- and ourselves

Chapter 8
The Scotts Letters: "One Man's Opinion"

As we moved from "Sharing Some Thoughts" into such important topics as the mutual responsibilities of the company and its associates, a second set of letters evolved. This new series, "One Man's Opinion," focused on the uniqueness of Scotts people and our relationship to one another. These messages are included here in two sections: "How We Work Together" and "Inside Ourselves."

"How We Work Together"

Scotts started from an excellent foundation: the concept of Associates, not employees. But as the company grew, so did the challenges to this philosophy, forcing us to consciously decide how we would continue to treat each other.

As important as all the tangible things were that we did at Scotts, they simply were not enough to sustain an environment of mutual respect and appreciation. An intangible thing was required: the desire of every person in the company to make a caring, mutually supportive spirit come into being.

We looked for every opportunity to make this happen. For example, one unusual program that we created seemed to touch people more deeply than our recreational facilities, health care programs, profit-sharing plan, or any of the other tangible benefits.

Every manager knows the importance of visiting the hospital or home when an associate is ill or suffers a family tragedy. But too often, we just don't have the time. To be sure the company was always there in times of trouble, we asked a Scotts retiree named Hazel Tossey if she would visit to help our people in any way possible. Hazel, a warm and outgoing person who had been the hostess at The Scott House (our guest house), was wonderful in this position. In a very literal way, she put a human face on the company. Sometimes she was able to help worried family members resolve questions or concerns, but her simply being there said, "We care about you."

Hazel benefited as well. Though she initially resisted taking on this responsibility, accepting it brought her out of an unexciting retirement to begin a whole new life. She almost literally became part of each family, everybody's grandmother, holding their hands and doing whatever she could to help. If something needed to be done that couldn't be accomplished through normal channels, she would pick up the phone and call me. For someone who had feared she was not equipped to do what it took, she created a wonderful role that evolved beyond any preconception.

During my tenure as CEO, there was more positive feedback from this simple outreach effort than from any of the expensive benefit programs. And of all the things that happened at Scotts, I loved this the most. It was a way of reminding people that we were all part of a family who tried to look after each other. That was a key point I tried to make in the letters on this subject.

"Inside Ourselves"

The next messages represent an abrupt change in direction. They are designed to make people think about themselves, about their work and their life.

By addressing such topics as "The Joy of Work" and "Standing Alone," we hoped to stimulate each Scotts Associate to think about his or her own character. Personal qualities, personal differences, personal attitudes: this is the territory explored in these inward-focused letters.

Getting value from these letters

Directionally, these letters represent the kind of messages that need to be said in many organizations. If you read them with an eye toward developing a similar program at your own company, you will probably find you are instinctively comfortable with some of them. Others may require struggle and thought. And some may not seem to fit your situation at all.

They were not written all at once, but represent an evolution of thought over several years. For this reason, my suggestion would be not to consume them too quickly. Give yourself time to consider a letter after you have absorbed it. Would this particular message apply to your company? If not, what is different about your situation? How would you approach it? You may find your thinking is stimulated, helping you create letters that are on target for your organization.

How We Work Together

How do we treat each other?

Part of my immediate love affair with Scotts was discovering its remarkably harmonious culture, strong work ethic, and rich heritage. I felt immediately that these were aspects of Scotts' character that should be protected and helped to grow.

Soon enough, despite our 100 years of small-town heritage, there came a point when a union drive forced us to ask ourselves what kind of company this was to be. Few of our Associates knew first-hand what unionization could mean. But having headed a company that had experienced union difficulties for a decade or more before rebuilding itself in a nonunion environment, I knew how hostile a management/labor split could become.

Would Scotts continue to be a place where people respected each other and worked as partners, or a place where they confronted each other from opposite sides of the table? Did our Associates want to work for a company where they could know that someone cared and that their efforts were important? Or did they want Scotts to be just another place to draw a paycheck?

I am proud of the fact that despite attempts to unionize Scotts, our people voted "no" each time. But each attempt was nerve-wracking, a reminder that we could never stop challenging ourselves to bring the Associate concept to life and make it meaningful.

The nature of a good company — like that of a good person — is that it tries to keep becoming better. So these letters express an attitude toward the Associate relationship that is only partly achievement. The other part is aspiration.

Messages about your own company's work environment may be difficult to write, but they are likely to be among the most important in your entire program. Because we have all seen so much rose-colored prose on this topic, it can be easy to slip into vague and meaningless clichés ("We provide a supportive environment that empowers employees to succeed professionally and personally. . ."). It's important to keep trying until you feel you have expressed yourself clearly and honestly.

"We Associates: Part I"

Long before "associate" became a common term for "employee," everyone at Scotts was an Associate. If the meaning is really lived, it changes the whole dynamics of a company. Associates come together as partners, as friends, as companions. That's what this word means to me.

In a company without an Associate heritage, transitioning to this concept may not be easy. It should start with the recognition that each person is both essential to and dependent on everyone else, and that everyone — from bottom to top — deserves to be treated with fairness, dignity, and respect.

 ## We Associates (Part I)

Several years ago the state of Ohio had a campaign going to attract new businesses, under the slogan of "Profit is not a dirty word in Ohio." That line has always intrigued me with its rally-round-the-flag implications, showing how heated a controversy is raging over the topic of a company's proper business objective. Many times, the inevitable conclusion seems to be that it's "them" versus "us"; either people <u>must</u> be getting a raw deal if the company's making money; or profitability will surely go down the drain if attention is paid to enriching people's work experience.

I just don't believe in that "either/or" conclusion. I'd go even

farther than that: I'd say that for a company to take full advantage
of its potential in the human and economic community it belongs
to, it <u>must</u> be able to combine both concepts: profitability and
individual fulfillment. The successful balancing of these two
objectives is one of the toughest jobs a company's leader can
have. I consider it one of the biggest ongoing challenges I face
here at Scotts... but I have a significant advantage to work with
– something that makes it possible for us to be both a people-
oriented family, and a profit-oriented, $100-million-plus
business enterprise.

That "something" is the fact that Scotts does not really have
1,200 employees. We have 1,200 <u>associates</u>.

What's the difference? To my mind, there's a clear distinction
between the two words. An employee can't exist without an
employer; right away the potential is there for polarization of
viewpoints and of interests, and we're back to the barricades
with "us" versus "them." In contrast, there is an equality of
value between one "associate" and another, with a strong bond
of common purpose linking them. I see that purpose as being
the desire to excel and be rewarded for excellence.

Any associate has the right to personal fulfillment, no matter
what his position. In this 1,200-strong voluntary family, we've
come together for essentially one reason: we want our association
with each other to enrich us, develop our potential, give us a
sense of accomplishment and the material rewards that go with
it. Our motives are frankly selfish... we expect our association
with Scotts to bring each of us more value than we could obtain
anywhere else, or on our own.

But a tremendous thing happens when an associate works with
other associates toward his own enrichment, development, and
accomplishment: he makes it easier for the people he works with
to grow, and he makes it possible for the family to succeed. Each
thing each one of us does is important to the rest of us and to the
total, and each of us is critical to the success of the total.

This kind of interrelationship doesn't happen by edict. It can be supported and nourished by a company's leaders; yet in the end it's not a question of leaders or followers, but of 1,200 individuals who really want to excel, to make the best possible use of the potential each of us has been given. The determination to fulfill our potential is, I believe, the most powerful single resource we can use to trigger our own personal growth and the growth of our company.

That brings up another question: what about Scotts, the company? Does the "family" have a responsibility toward the associates who are helping it to profit through their efforts? Yes, of course it does: and that responsibility is the counterweight in this finely tuned balance. I'd like to spend a little time exploring this area with you in the next memo.

This is a difficult subject to write about... one of the most complex and one of the most important that I want to discuss with you. Books and books have been published on the theory of the individual and the corporation, but it is rare for a company to try to define exactly what it wants that relationship to be in reality.

Quite simply, all I've been saying is that Scotts' associate concept depends on every one of us – that means me, and it means you. You and I gain directly from its success; and by making it succeed, we help the entire Scotts family to take advantage of our full potential. I greatly prefer that team effort to a partisan battlefield where nobody can hear beyond his own war-cry, whether it is "profit" or "people." It's only with profit and people together that we can expect to succeed.

"We Associates: Part II"

The central feature of the Associate philosophy is inspiration and encouragement of individuals to do their best. This comes about when Associates feel they are an integral part of the business, their thoughts are welcome, and their contribution is respected and rewarded. In other words, a company has responsibilities to its Associates just as Associates have responsibilities to the company.

If either party defaults on its obligations, this implicit contract is broken. To cite a flagrant example, if a company increases executive bonuses while cutting workers' pay, a fundamental sense of trust is lost. Cooperation can turn to opposition, and antagonisms arise.

Just because a business has been in existence for years, there is no guarantee that it will still be there next month or next year. As many companies have discovered the hard way, the true worth of the Associate concept is most evident when it ceases to exist.

 ## We Associates (Part II)

A few days ago I happened to be discussing the ins and outs of Scotts' associate concept with a good friend of mine, and I shared with him the frustrations I was feeling in trying to do justice to this very emotional and complex subject in these memos. My friend, who is the head of a company we do business with, said with frankness, "Yes, it's so much easier just to strike out the word 'employee' and write in 'associate' instead. And so many companies I know just leave it at that."

How much easier it would be just to pay lip service to the associate concept. You know, it's much less time-consuming to tell someone exactly what to do than to spend hours encouraging him to take the initiative himself. It's much less bruising to hide in a corner and just "do your job" the same way, day after day, than to struggle to keep doing it better and faster and more proudly. So why are we trying to do it the hard way?

For one thing, the personal rewards are greater. An associate relationship is a two-way street – when you excel at your job you're helping a lot of other people to excel at theirs; when <u>they</u> perform well, they make it easier for you to perform. This interrelationship, or interdependency, is really the spirit of our associate philosophy. And its result is a far greater potential for personal growth and reward than the traditional employer/ employee outlook permits.

But along with this opportunity to grow comes a greater responsibility. An employee can always say, "Well, I can't help such-and-such; that's not my job." (In fact, the word "employ" simply means "to make use of"; it doesn't really imply any initiative on the part of whomever you've employed.) But an associate can't hide behind that one-way-street sign, because he knows he <u>can</u> help it – and not only that, but he <u>has</u> to help it if he's going to do his job right and give others the opportunity to do theirs. There are no excuses in an associate business, not on any level; I can't hide from my responsibility to my fellow associates any better than you can. Not if I'm serious about the value that I intend to gain for myself out of the association.

The word "associate" is long-standing terminology here at Scotts; and the sense of this company as a family certainly dates back to the days when it was run by a real family: O.M., Dwight, and Hubert Scott. It's the successful combination of these two concepts – the family and the associate – that has allowed us to develop the kind of working environment that people can grow in. Like a family, the company has a responsibility to protect, support, and reward the people who have gathered together to become its "family members"; and those people, the associates, have a reciprocal responsibility to help the family unit as a whole succeed. The result: when the company performs well, its associates should profit; when associates perform well, the company should profit.

These are the counterbalancing responsibilities I mentioned briefly in the last memo. In addition to the tangible elements of fulfillment, there are all the intangibles that are part of providing a satisfying work environment. Determining the right levels of all these variables isn't a very simple job, as you may know, and the irony of it is that there's never a moment when you can step back and brush off your hands and say, "Well, that's that!" – because it's never completed; a company has to keep working at it continuously. We could be the best-paying company in the state of Ohio with the best benefits package there is, but if we didn't have a working environment that let people develop their potential, I'd consider that we had failed our associates. Conversely, we could have a terrific working environment, but if our compensation plan didn't reward people for their contributions to the company's growth, we'd have failed just as badly.

So, we keep working on it. And in the process, I like to think that we're breathing more life day by day into that word "associate." Like any other term, it can be misused or misinterpreted – but the implications it brings are so significant that you'll rarely see the word "employee" used in this company. Our associate concept is what makes us succeed as a family; it's what produces the creative friction that sparks great ideas; it's what gives each of us the opportunity to grow and to help others grow. And the more each of us lives up that concept, the farther we will go – as individuals, and as a company.

"No Time Clocks"

In most manufacturing businesses, the first thing you see at the entrance to the shop floor is a time clock. Scotts' three manufacturing plants had none.

This was a mystery to many newcomers, including some from our parent company. No time clocks? How could we be sure people were actually working when they were supposed to?

My answer to these puzzled questions was that, like so many other issues at Scotts, the answer was trust. We believed that most people's response to being trusted is "If you have high expectations of me, I'll try not to let you down."

Why should the honest majority suffer for the possible wrong behavior of a very few individuals? Suppose two percent of Associates took advantage of our trust. Would it be right to make the other 98 percent feel their word was not good enough?

You may want to look at your own company in this light. Do your practices and policies trust workers to do the right thing, or do they assume that everyone is like the misguided "two percent"?

 ## No Time Clocks

There are no time clocks at Scotts. And I hope never to see any on our premises. Time clocks often are an excuse some companies use to avoid having to think about trust. Such companies may shrug and say, "The Government makes me put them in," or "We have to have precise records"… but more often than not, whatever reason they finally give is really a rationalization for the fact that they don't think they can trust their people.

From the first day you walk in the door at Scotts, your word is trusted. Your signature, at the bottom of the weekly time card you fill out, is the substantiation of your work. It's as simple as that.

We couldn't live up to our own beliefs if it were any other way.

After all, an essential part of the trust that exists at Scotts is the conviction that people are fundamentally trust-<u>worthy</u>, that when they are treated with respect they'll respond in a way that makes you respect them all the more. As you know, this is exactly the philosophy that lies behind our "No-Quibble" guarantee: we are so committed to the belief that our customers will live up to our expectations of their honesty and integrity, that we base our entire refund policy on the customer's word.

This philosophy of ours startles many visitors from outside our company. Frequently they'll ask, "Don't people take advantage of it?" Yes, there are occasional instances when our trust is abused – by customers, and by Associates. But in the long run, it's this rare individual who does abuse it who is the loser, not the company. Dishonesty is always a conscious action; and there's something inside each of us that dislikes breaking faith with others, and makes us feel a little worse for not having lived up to someone else's high expectation of us.

I hope it will never be the case at Scotts that we give up our trust in the majority of people because of the actions of a thoughtless few. If that day should ever come, for whatever reason, we will be on the way to losing the basic spirit of our Associate relationship... because it's only a short step from the absence of trust to the absence of respect for personal dignity.

And then we're no longer individual Associates in an enterprise – we're just numbers on a time clock.

"Style vs. Results"

Gone were the days when most managers at Scotts were promoted from within. The company's growth increasingly compelled us to hire men and women with experience at other companies, often with MBAs or other formal training.

As these new people joined our homegrown managers, somewhat of a culture clash ensued. Some managers had a more rigorous and impersonal style; others a more easygoing style. Was it better to be a "tough guy" or a "nice guy"?

In this letter, we tried to move the discussion to a different level. The issue wasn't whether one management style was better than another, but the importance of caring enough — in a businesslike way — to help one's team achieve the best possible results.

 Style vs. Results

Is it really true that nice guys don't win ball games?

An associate of ours ended by asking himself that question not too long ago. He was upset because he'd always considered himself a "good" manager: he had given his people free rein to use their creativity, without trying to direct them or breathe over their shoulders. To his surprise, he'd discovered that not only were many of them unhappy with this style of supervision, but the work was disappointing. He said to me, "I guess I'll just have to get tough. No more 'Mr. Nice Guy': it doesn't get results."

In my experience, his conclusion is partly right… but, even more importantly, it's also partly wrong. I believe that it is possible to be gentle, kind and considerate and still get results – but the magic ingredient is "caring." Caring about the results, and caring about the people whose effort is vital to the results.

Many of us think of Vince Lombardi as the classic example of a "tough guy" – a hard-driving, win-at-all-costs manager. Yet the quote I remember best from Lombardi is "Nothing but the best is acceptable" – and he cared tremendously about the individual team members who were so important in meeting his expectation of "the best." He didn't stand back remotely and fold his arms (like our misguided associate) and say, "Okay, fellows, how you win the game is up to you; I'll just watch." Neither did he make all the decisions; he didn't dot every "i" and cross every "t" for them. He let them know what great things he believed they were capable of, and he helped them to accomplish those results, taking advantage of his own experience, skill, and instinct. This, in my book, is caring.

With this ingredient, nice guys <u>can</u> win ball games. Your manner can be low-key and firm, without being either remote or wishy-washy; if people know what you expect of them and how to do it, I don't believe you have to scream and pound the table and humiliate them to get it. Furthermore, in the long run, intimidation as a management style tends to backfire on the user: intimidated people usually withdraw their talents and energies until they're only doing what it takes to get by. True, you'll get a result – but it'll meet your minimum standards, not your maximum. (Someone once summed up this effect as "Expect the best of me and you'll get it; expect the worst, and you won't be disappointed.")

On the other hand, if people feel comfortable that you want to help them succeed, they'll be more interested in helping <u>you</u>. That's true, I believe, no matter what level of the company you're on. If you're a manager, you have the added responsibility of judging results – which means that exercising fairness is a large part of a manager's caring. Being a "nice guy" doesn't mean that you tolerate slipshod work or condone mistakes, but that you care enough to figure out why they happen when they do, and help to solve the problems that caused them instead of shrugging indifferently or blowing your top.

Our associate's mistake, it seems to me, was in confusing being a careless manager with being a "nice guy". A really caring manager <u>is</u> a nice guy… but he or she is also tough, demanding nothing but the best and setting a personal example of what that standard means.

Any other approach will not only fail to draw out the best in each individual and in the team as a unit… but it also may well end by fouling up the whole ball game.

"Respecting, and Being Respected"

In my view, there were two requirements to hold a management job at Scotts. The first was to have the technical skills for the job. The second was to have a respect for people — a willingness to treat them with dignity, to put oneself in the other person's place and ask, "How would I feel?", to admit free and open constructive criticism that could allow the company to improve.

The first one can be acquired. But the people skill — it's in the gut, right down in the bottom of the stomach. It has to be part of you all the time; you can't turn it on and off.

To managers who just didn't "get it," the following letter was a tactful way to suggest, "If you don't have this kind of gut feeling, will you please go work for a company that doesn't demand it?"

 Respecting, and Being Respected

The most destructive force in society is the one which subtly encourages us to disregard each other's dignity and worth. Although this impulse can be encouraged by outside influences, its roots already exist in all of us, inviting us to label each other as "different" in conveniently abstract terms – conservative or liberal, labor or management, hard-hat or hippie, members of this or that economic, political, religious, or ethnic group. The end result is we aren't compelled to admit to other human beings that we are human too.

As a result, we frequently find ourselves struggling in inflexible opposition with others, instead of working in harmony with them to achieve a common purpose. When a manager wonders out loud if he is being weak by being considerate of the rest of his team – as we discussed in the last letter – we see a startling example of this alienating force at work.

However, managers don't have a monopoly on destructiveness. It's just as easy for any team member to wreak havoc with the team's work, by being insensitive to the basic human need for respect. In "Style vs. Results," we looked at what disciplines a team manager must exercise to help the team to run smoothly... and, in actual fact, <u>every</u> team member has those same responsibilities:

<u>First</u>, to be aware of and to care about other team members as individuals, with their own need for respect.

<u>Second</u>, to care about the excellence of what the team does – and to try to live up to that standard in personal performance.

When all of the team's members believe in these disciplines and live up to them, what results is a productive and enjoyable work environment. Respect is a tremendously powerful force; it can break down walls between individuals who had been in opposition, and it can break through the artificially low ceiling a group or individual may have set on its own growth.

Admittedly, perfect harmony and unity is an ideal. Sometimes the raw material won't be quite right to begin with: a team member may refuse to get involved in the effort, may communicate indifference or antagonism instead of respect, or may act in a way that limits others' respect for him or her. But no matter what the circumstances, the absence of discipline in one team member never justifies its absence in others. In personal experience, I've seen that attempting to deal autocratically with people only makes problems worse. On the other hand, the effort of working together to resolve indifferences can often help to build the unity a team needs.

One of our Associates noted in his own thoughts about this topic, "Respect makes a team out of two people." Those two people – or twenty, or twelve hundred – may be totally different individuals, with different talents, different abilities, different personalities... and yet they are alike in being valuable to each other's success.

Respecting, and being respected, are crucial elements in any true Associate relationship. For that reason, I hope we always will try to make them characteristic of Scotts.

Dealing with problems

Someone asked me once how to know if people trust you. I don't think it can be defined in tangible terms. It may be as simple as a look in people's eyes, or the guardedness of their language when you interact. With experience, you can learn to recognize it (though not always).

Once there is a relationship of trust, it's possible to discuss any subject in your letters. In particular, you can talk about negative things with credibility. People will be more open to hearing you because you have already laid the groundwork and established your vulnerability.

This can be tremendously valuable when an issue arises that everyone needs to be aware of, as our experience at Scotts demonstrated.

"Petitions"

A few years after the letter program began, some Associates prepared a petition that eventually made its way to my office. The subject is no longer important; but the petition itself was a concern on a couple of levels.

First of all, a petition is something you might submit to attract the attention of a king or a czar, not a leader who is already predisposed to act in your best interest. More importantly, what kind of message does it send when you take two seconds to scrawl your signature on a petition? If a problem in the company is bothering you, don't you have a responsibility to stand up and say so? Scotts was not the kind of company where people lost their jobs for speaking out in good faith.

The following letter, "Petitions," was written and sent quickly, while the petition itself was fresh in people's minds. Because of the foundation we had already laid with letters about the Associate concept, it is likely that many more Associates understood and appreciated this message than if it had come out of the blue.

 ## Petitions

Several of our associates recently had raised the question of petitions and their use to express a broadly held opinion of any group of associates. Their contention was that this was not only an appropriate but perhaps the only way for associates to express their viewpoint.

If petitions truly expressed the desires of those signing I would have to agree they have their place, but experience shows this is rarely the case. Petitions normally express the interest of a few people who then get others to sign their names. Most of us sign petitions because of peer pressure. It is not comfortable to say "no" to someone you have to work with everyday and besides, "I may need their help in the future." It is, also, easy to rationalize by telling yourself, "If I'm not strongly opposed to the petition, there is no harm in signing – it really doesn't make any difference to me one way or the other."

My experience tells me petitions rarely express the <u>real</u> viewpoint of all the signers. Fortunately, there are better ways for us to express our viewpoint and ask questions. They are:

1. Talk to our Supervisor or Manager;

2. Talk to Associate Relations;

3. Use the Feedback Forms – assures confidentiality, if this is important;

4. Use the "Open Door Policy" with Senior Management.

Not everyone will agree with my viewpoint, but you have a right to know how I feel. When I hear from an associate or several associates individually on any subject, I listen carefully and try to take appropriate action. When I receive a petition, I immediately wonder who is trying to push their viewpoint by pressuring other to sign a petition. One of Scotts' most important strengths is the opportunity for each associate to speak for himself and be heard.

Inside Ourselves

The heart of the matter

Without the creativity and ingenuity of motivated individuals, a company's tangible assets — its plant, equipment, inventory, and so on — can't create success. Granted, technology can make a process more efficient. But when was the last time a computer thought up an innovation that would improve the customer experience? Only a team of inspired, dedicated people can keep creating better plans and better products to help a company succeed over the long term.

Leaders have tremendous influence over this process because they define the company's expectations. Sooner or later, people will meet these expectations. If you don't expect much, or expect the worst, that's what you will get. But if you expect the best, and show your willingness to help your team members attain it, there is no limit to what they can accomplish.

People's attitude toward their work is truly "the heart of the matter." Do they know what you expect of them? The following letters may give you some ideas for messages of your own.

"Footprints"

It has always seemed to me that a company achieves excellence only by virtue of the excellence of its people. The most important advantage of this letter program was the ability to speak to people one by one, encouraging them to step out of the crowd and stand up for their beliefs.

One by one, quality individuals create a quality company.

 Footprints

Many people work hard to be invisible. By their definition, it's the road to security – not to make waves, not to call attention to themselves, not to run the risk of doing anything wrong.

What is especially startling to me is to find that among this group are many people not only with talent but also with college educations, and even advanced degrees. I sense an attitude among some that says, "I've put in my years at school; now it's business's job to see that I work my way up to president. And if that doesn't happen – why, it's not my fault; it's the company's fault." And then these invisible people sit back and wait complacently for opportunity to knock.

Well, opportunity knocks darn seldom for those who deprive themselves of chances to demonstrate excellence.

It's true that company structure can sometimes seem to be an obstacle to personal success, with its reviews and requests and all the trappings. Unfortunately, one of the facts of business life is that size begets structure, so that problem can't be completely eliminated. But an individual who wants to succeed, can succeed, in spite of the structure – not by dealing in internal politics, but by trying to be above the ordinary. Structure is not a reason for mediocrity, only an excuse.

I believe the way to advance, in this company at least, is to be so good at what you do whatever it may be that the opportunity will come looking for you. In other words, make yourself visible. Opportunity isn't equipped with X-ray vision, to single you out in the middle of the crowd. And believe me, Scotts needs people who not only are outstanding, but also have the desire and motivation to succeed.

Speaking practically, in my years of business I can't recall a situation where there was as much opportunity as there is in this company today. It took us 106 years to reach our first $100 million in sales; it should take us 7 years to reach the second hundred million. That growth offers tremendous potential within Scotts, for people who are eager, interested, ready, and willing to take advantage of it.

As we try to identify those individuals who will play a major part in Scotts' future, what I continually look for – and what I expect other members of management to look for – are footprints: the marks of contributed value that some people leave behind as they move through their day-to-day responsibilities. I'd like to see more of you become visible and make innovative contributions. This company deserves the best that your mind and talents can offer... and you owe it to yourself to exercise and develop them.

Think boldly. Shrug off excuses. And make FOOTPRINTS!

"The Joy of Work"

Does it come as a shock to see the words "joy" and "work" in the same phrase? They may even seem incompatible.

We spend more of our lives at work than in any other pursuit. If we don't cross the bridge that connects work to joy, what does that say about us? Who wants to admit they're spending most of their life doing something that doesn't feed them?

When work does become a joy, the rewards are priceless. Unlike material possessions, which do not bring real happiness and can indeed become a tyranny, the personal fulfillment that comes from putting our talents to work repays us in many ways, over and over.

 ## The Joy of Work

One of the things that's made Scotts what it is today is that we've been blessed, on all levels of the company, with people who understand and appreciate the joy of work.

I wish I could be sure that my children and my grandchildren will be able to continue to understand and appreciate this special pleasure. The increasing problem seems to be that we seem to be living at a time when "work" has become a four-letter word, a necessary evil that must be endured in order to enjoy ourselves afterward. Mentioning "joy" and "work" in the same breath just isn't done – after all, isn't work supposed to be drudgery?

The result is that there's growing pressure against working hard, against being conscientious, curious, and creative in work. We see this pressure on our children in school, as well as on ourselves on the job: people are made to feel uncomfortable, even somewhat freakish, if they really fully give themselves to their work and try to create something better than the norm. It's far more comfortable for many to go along with the crowd and slack off... but this takes a serious toll in demolished self-respect.

It can't help but be demoralizing to squander your precious time and energy in just "getting by."

To my mind, this unhealthy philosophy defies the belief that all of us arrived on this earth with God-given talents. The self-fulfillment that comes from creating value and meaning with these talents is really what work is all about – and it is a basic part of life. Our leisure time, on the other hand, serves to let us restore our talents and energies. In other words, instead of talking about a "means" (work) and an "end" (leisure), it seems to me that we're really talking about two halves of a truly whole, happy, creative human being.

When I began to think and act this way, I found out that there's no such thing as drudgery – because we were born to create, not to stagnate. And there's no such thing as retirement either, because the creative process can continue as long as we live, whether the job framework is there or not. (I have an 82-year-old father, and I don't think he's retired yet!)

Remember, we were born to create, not to stagnate. If you have a sense of stagnation, it's time to think through what you could be bringing enjoyably and productively to your work, and to determine how you could develop and strengthen those talents.

We're created, each one of us, with certain gifts we had no voice in choosing... but in our lives, we have the opportunity to discover and develop those gifts through our work, and thus to recreate ourselves. That, I believe, is the real "joy of work."

"Hearts and Minds"

The older I get, the more I am convinced that nothing important happens until our emotions are engaged.

For example, think of the many logical appeals to quit smoking — the Surgeon General's warnings, notices on cigarette packages, and so forth. But when people do successfully kick the habit, it's an emotional decision. In my own case, faced one day with having to drop what I was doing to run out and buy more cigarettes, I looked at the empty package and said, "Who's running my life — me or that?" I never smoked again.

People won't invest their emotions in something unless they have a sense of owning it and are willing to make themselves vulnerable. In "Hearts and Minds," we addressed the value of emotional involvement, and its implications for managers.

 ## Hearts and Minds

In many years of working life, I've been struck by one particular quality shared by everyone who is really happy in his or her job. It's a quality we all recognize, and often underestimate, in ourselves and in others. I'm referring to the importance of the heart.

All of us understand the tangible rewards from work: salary, fringe benefits, and so forth. We know that, in all likelihood, we can earn those rewards just by being physically present on the job and making reasonable use of our minds. But in my own experience, I've seen what enormous intangible joy and rewards come to an individual from deeper involvement – from committing not just your mind but also your heart to the work you do.

Our language is rich in expressions relating to enthusiastic involvement: pitching in "wholeheartedly," "putting your heart into it," trying "with all your heart." I don't for a minute believe this is coincidental. The heart is tremendously important to getting a sense of success and self-fulfillment out of work. In fact, I don't really feel anybody can be what they're capable of being until they've taken the step of becoming emotionally involved in their work.

In making this point, I don't mean to suggest that people should be burning the midnight oil constantly or turning into workaholics. We're simply talking about bringing more creative energy, more involvement, to the job. The reward should be a personal enrichment of life, both at work and outside of work.

Some managers, unfortunately, underestimate the importance of their people's hearts. These managers seem to feel that they've done their job if they deal objectively and decisively with an issue, without bothering to address its peripheral emotional aspects... which often are more important to the whole team's success.

Simply "managing the work" is sterile and, in the long run, self-defeating unless caring is part of the process – caring about the other people involved, caring about the excellence of what the team is doing. In other words, managers cannot manage well with mind alone. And as they move up within a company, whatever other credentials they bring to their jobs, they must be involved personally and emotionally to a greater and greater extent. After all, when you're guiding a living, growing organization made up of dozens or hundreds of human beings, it's not enough only to be able to think; you also have to be able to feel. That's where the heart comes in.

Admittedly, not everyone can make a full commitment to try to work with both mind and heart. For those who can, I believe there's an intangible reward, the joy of work, which grows with the depth of involvement. When you've worked wholeheartedly to make something succeed – when you've sweated over it, wrestled with it, believed in it, fought for it, and maybe prayed a little for it – then you become part of it, and it becomes part of you. Whether or not what you have undertaken does succeed, you've created something from yourself – and that's a reward that those who stay aloof and uninvolved can never know.

"Wishful Doing"

We knew that some people would argue against particular messages in this series because "it's not like that now." It's important to acknowledge when reality is not exactly as pictured, but remember that you are trying to create the way you would like things to be. Unless your dreams are written down, how will people know whether there is any progress toward them?

That said, we have to recognize that ideals are usually unreachable. There will probably never be a day when everyone works in perfect harmony, feeling completely content, emotionally fulfilled, and amply rewarded. But that doesn't mean we should not aspire to see that day.

 Wishful Doing

I have a confession to make to you.

Deep inside I am a wishful thinker, an aspirer. A basic part of the zest in my life comes from wishing for better and greater things than what I see around me, and from trying to make these things happen.

Let me make an educated guess about you – deep inside you're the same, aren't you?

As these "One Man's Opinion" letters have progressed, some associates have been frank enough to point out gaps between my observations and what they themselves perceive as really happening at Scotts. Many of their colleagues, for example, don't experience "the joy of work." Not all of their leaders really succeed in "respecting and being respected." Some of their most talented and intelligent co-workers would rather snipe anonymously at other people's decisions, instead of emerging to make "footprints" of their own.

Le Herron, you sure are out of touch with today's reality.

Yes, I do know that gaps exist. There is indeed a difference between some of the things that happen today, and what wishful thinkers like you and I might like to see instead. Our aspirations toward better things – whether we hold them out as goals, ideals, or dreams – are what we each strive to fulfill over a period of time, recognizing that there will probably always be some shortcomings, some gap between the desirable and the real. But should one give up the attempt to reach an ideal simply because it may not be completely attainable? What's important in life is not perfection, but progress towards perfection. Isn't there value in trying one's best to narrow the gap?

It appears to me, as we consider this question, that wishful <u>doing</u> is far more important that simply wishful thinking. The gaps I detect at Scotts are the chief reason for many actions I have taken and will take, and they are a major motive for these letters.

In "One Man's Opinion" I don't really intend to report on today's reality, but rather to help shape tomorrow's, by sharing my beliefs to encourage you and your own ideals and wishes. To the fullest extent possible, I aspire to see you too become a "wishful doer," if you are not one already. In your own aspirations, you hold the key to make better and greater things happen; you can become too positive a force to be defeated by negative thinkers and negative doers, or to be tyrannized by gaps between the way things are and the way you sense they should be.

Wishing, dreaming, aspiring, together I hope we can narrow those gaps... until they vanish.

Confronting challenges

Adversity is a powerful force in shaping character, and battling it is one of the most effective ways to learn about ourselves. Every challenge is an opportunity to test the strength of our principles. Sometimes it also helps us discover what those principles are.

What if circumstances inside or outside your company demand that you act against your beliefs? The best advice I've been able to give younger people is the same counsel that I was given years ago, when I was stepping into a CEO position for the first time.

My wife and I had relocated and had bought a house, so we were appreciably in debt. My departing predecessor, who had become my mentor and selected me to succeed him, said one of the wisest things I have ever heard in my years in business. "Young man," he told me, "make yourself financially independent."

He went on to explain that he didn't mean for me to become wealthy, but to put enough in the bank to be able to bridge a period if I should lose my job. By removing the fear of being without a paycheck, this would allow me to say and do what I felt was right.

How large a nest egg does it take to become financially independent? There's no universal answer. It's tied to how long you could survive financially if you lost your job.

Betty and I followed this advice. If we hadn't, it's doubtful that my career would have gone anywhere. Becoming financially independent enabled me to stand up for what I believed in, even if it was unpopular at the time.

It's saddening to see so many capable individuals spending the next paycheck before they get it, and being prevented by their debt from being their own person. If your company takes a position you don't agree with, or it has no position on a subject you feel strongly about, you can't let yourself be controlled by fear of losing your job.

Real progress in my career happened only when I stood up for something that could have gotten me fired. When you have to surrender your principles to protect your job, it is quite possible to end up with neither.

"How Can a Problem Be Good for You?"

Many people avoid problems. They would rather play it safe, even though it denies them opportunities to grow. Their life becomes controlled by a desire to avoid embarrassment and disappointment.

Fear of failure may be more pervasive than we suspect. But one thing is worse than failing: not trying. This is a cardinal sin, one of the worst forms of cheating yourself.

The biggest part of fear of failure is worry about what our peers will think. But what will they think if we don't even try? And what does it say about us, if we suppress our beliefs and abilities because we are afraid to stand up for them?

Avoiding problems in order to live more comfortably is a sure way to limit the possibilities for yourself. If there's one thing I would wish for my children and grandchildren, it is a willingness to look problems in the eye and try to solve them. Failing to try is far worse than failing to succeed.

 How Can a Problem Be Good for You?

There's a line in a popular song that tells us, "I never promised you a rose garden." Isn't it strange, though, that we spend most of our lives believing that if we could only be truly successful at what we do, life <u>would</u> be a rose garden... no problems, no tough decisions. In fact, it seems we often think that to be beset by problems means we've somehow failed (if we'd done things right, nothing would have gone wrong).

I would like to say flatly that I think this is ridiculous. The only people who have no problems are those who have no goals – for what's a problem but a stumbling block between us and some goal we're trying to reach? Furthermore, problems can actually help us reach those goals, depending on how we handle them.

It seems to me that a problem can be just as valuable in building will and character as physical exercise is in building bodily health and strength. Like exercise, a problem is an often unwelcome discipline: given our choice, there are plenty of things higher on everybody's list of priorities than struggling with adversity. And yet, I know in hindsight that the times in my life that have been the most value to me have been those that were the most trying and horrendously difficult.

A problem takes on value because of the personal reward an individual gets from dealing with it. It can bring us emotional maturity, mental broadening and development. It can even help build a sense of confidence. Part of the security of age, I've found, comes from one's experience of a broad range of problems; new problems are often just derivatives of old ones we've already encountered.

You've probably heard the cliché about a problem being an opportunity in disguise. What does this mean – an opportunity to look good in front of the boss? That seems to suggest that the only time a problem benefits us is when (and if) we solve it, which is like saying that the only way you benefit from training for a marathon is if you win it. The exercise of will and character in itself strengthens us, even if uncontrollable circumstances prevent us from obtaining precisely the results we would like. A problem, in other words, is an opportunity to become a stronger human being.

Fear of failure, then, isn't a valid reason to run away from problems. If you are true to yourself, if you know what your goals are, you'll find that problems are inevitable; the only way to really fail at a problem is to put blinders on and sidle past it, refusing to get involved with it.

I don't mean to say that sitting and stewing about difficulties will necessarily be beneficial… in fact, to worry unproductively can be very destructive. Dealing successfully with a problem really demands the effort of our God-given intelligence and energy, and most importantly, the <u>will</u> to reach that important goal which is now threatened. Fretting, without acting, is like trying to get into shape by thinking about exercise.

There is one wonderfully consoling quality common to all problems: they will pass. They're temporary. And if, knowing that, you can grab hold of a problem and say, "I'm going to learn something from dealing with this pain in the neck," I think that you're just that much closer to achieving the goals you cherish.

"Standing Alone"

People who can't afford to lose their jobs often hesitate to make waves. It would seem that a company's leaders should be exempt from this situation, but sometimes they are not. Pressured by an expensive lifestyle and favors owed, they may feel forced to go along with the board of directors on decisions they don't agree with.

Fear of becoming unpopular holds others back from taking a stand. To dissipate this fear, we need to help people learn to disagree with an idea without attacking the individual who suggested it. Some training in language skills may be required to make the person feel secure before moving on to discuss the issue at hand. ("I have tremendous respect for your experience, but I'm concerned that. . . .")

Try to overcome your hesitancy and pursue your convictions. Top management may not like your ideas, but if what you believe is on solid rock, it's hard to argue against it. That means you have a good chance of getting your views accepted. But you will never have a chance unless you are willing to stand alone.

 Standing Alone

From my perspective of nearly 40 years in business, there are two statements that appear to be unspoken rules of the American workplace. Considering that they're not advertised or openly applauded, they are remarkably pervasive and incredibly durable.

1. <u>Don't do any more than you have to.</u>
2. <u>Never say anything good about the company.</u>

And wherever this attitude thrives, in corporations or government agencies, it is tremendously corrosive. In return for the thrill of joining one's peers in underground opposition to "the boss," it transforms the workplace into a wasteland of sullen mediocrity, where personal excellence is unknown, extra effort is discouraged, and change comes only in bursts of bitter confrontation. If that sound far-fetched, you can see its cumulative effect for yourself, by looking at the nationwide sag in our productivity and our deteriorating competitive position in the world.

It exasperates me that we have to pay for this destructive attitude in shoddy and high-priced goods and services, as well as in greater anxiety about the chances of controlling our country's future. But most of all, it's frustrating that these ideas go unchallenged by those who have the most to gain from challenging them. Bright, talented, energetic people are allowing themselves to be persuaded into second-rate lives by the pressure of peers who want no comparison with their own mediocrity. "Hey!" a veteran whispers to the enterprising employee. "Don't work so hard! You want to make the rest of us look bad?"

What a waste! Why don't more people resist this poisonous wisdom? Why consent to cheat yourself of the opportunity to create wonderful things with your God-given talents, in return for a career of mediocrity hidden in the crowd? Why work so long in deceit and self-denial, when your natural ambitions would normally lead you to excel and prosper?

Of course, peer pressure is an awesome thing, especially when one has never had to resist it before. It's uncomfortable to stand alone. You might lose the comradeship of some of your peers... but do you suppose you may be grudgingly awarded their respect, instead?

You see, I can appreciate the benefits of standing alone from both sides. As a worker, I've stood alone more times than I would like to admit, not because of any fondness for controversy but because I didn't want to settle for less than what seemed to me to be right. Whatever one's popularity or lack of it, I believe this is the only way a person can really live at peace with himself.

On the other hand, as a manager responsible for numbers of workers, I cry out for more of you to stand alone. Let me see what imagination and skills you can bring to help this company better itself! Give us a chance to reward your ability and enthusiasm! No one can spot your talent if you camouflage it with mediocrity.

The trend, fortunately, seems to be reversing itself. Companies are beginning to re-emphasize excellence in work, shifting more of that responsibility directly to workers through concepts like the quality circle. However, the fundamental change really has to happen inside people, who decide that the will of the crowd is not as important as their own right to seek fulfillment of their goals. It's these individuals who will reap the greatest rewards during their working lives, in terms of self-respect, satisfaction, and material success. This potential is in all of us – if we're willing to risk breaking the rules which restrict us.

If doing your best means that no one will stand with you, stand alone! Stick to what you think is right. Just remember, you were born to create – not to stagnate!

Leadership

Leaders need people. And people need good leadership. No matter what our position is in the corporate family, we are equally important to each other.

If you are responsible for people in your company, you need to accept the idea that everybody has a unique talent. Your job is to recognize what that talent is and find a way to help the individual bring it forth.

Maybe Mary Smith isn't in the right job for her particular talent. Maybe Joe Jones hasn't found his own special talent yet.

The key to success as a leader isn't "Looking out for Number 1." It's looking out for the people you're responsible for, and making it possible for them to do their best. That is the only way to achieve your own goals.

In the following letters, we addressed two aspects of this relationship that have been in the headlines a great deal recently: the ego-driven leader, and the use and misuse of power.

"How to Succeed in Business"

One might be concerned that this message is dated. But evidence to the contrary can be found in current TV and press reports about CEOs whose zeal in "looking out for #1" has led to subpoenas, trials, and sentences.

Real leaders derive power not from serving their own ego, but from serving the interests of the people on whom their ultimate success — and their company's — depends. It wouldn't be so sad if these misguided CEOs were the only ones involved. But to a large extent, the people in their companies are their innocent victims.

 ## How to Succeed in Business

It concerns me that young people just coming into the work force are still being given a very peculiar idea of how to succeed on the job. Best-selling books like <u>Power</u>! and <u>Looking Out for Number #1</u> warn them that it's everyone for himself, and that they'll have to claw and gouge their way to the top. I'm sure you've heard this philosophy before; it sounds as if it must be true just because it's been around so long.

Yet trying to succeed on one's own is terribly difficult, if not impossible. For one thing, it takes a great deal of scheming, politicking, and maneuvering, which is tremendously hard work. And often the result of all this effort is that Number #1's co-workers, annoyed at being manipulated or shouldered aside, are only too glad to see him fall flat on his face. (In fact, they'll probably help to trip him.)

In short, an advancement policy based solely on looking out for one's self is not only arduous but probably doomed to disaster from the start. In my own experience, it's always seemed far simpler and easier to encourage other people to join me in working together for success, whose rewards we will all be able to share.

"Learning to work together with others" is probably the closest thing to a business success formula that I can conceive of. There's room in this formula for all the personal ambition you might have. Ambitious people working together will have a greater chance of attaining personal success, as their common enterprise succeeds. On the other hand, those who can't work together will probably end up sharing their failures together. (Imagine the difference if the forces in the auto industry, for example, had learned to work together instead of surviving only through confrontation.)

Of course, we can't control all the factors leading to success or failure, but by controlling how we go about trying to succeed – by sharing the effort with others, in return for sharing the rewards to come – we can certainly improve the odds in our favor. For instance, if I work hard to make Scotts succeed, solely so I myself can earn a better salary, my determination will have some effect on our success. But if the people responsible for research, manufacturing, marketing and distribution are working together with me so that all of us can earn more, we have a much better chance to succeed. If we can encourage that spirit to permeate the entire organization, Scotts becomes darn near unbeatable, and our chances of attaining success on a companywide basis become excellent. By sharing individually and collectively in the rewards of that success, we're all inspired to keep succeeding. That, I believe, is how people (and companies) really advance.

On a corporate level, Scotts has tried for many years to make a practice of sharing success with the people who have made it possible. Speaking from my own viewpoint, I take enormous joy in this sharing. When, after a year of companywide effort and record-breaking sales, I hear an Associate comment that the size of the company's profit sharing contribution means he'd receive the equivalent of 57 weeks of pay for a 52-week year, I am delighted by his pleasure. When I see new cars in the company lot, when I hear of new families which Scotts' shared rewards have helped in some way to launch, I know the true blessing of success.

If those misinformed young workers could stand in my shoes and feel the pride and satisfaction in my heart at that moment, I think they might understand a little more fully what it really means to succeed. I can't believe there's any joy in "looking out for Number #1" which compares with this.

"The Nature of Power"
"The Temptations of Power"

The difference between authority and power is one of the most important concepts in leading people, yet it is hardly ever discussed. If you are a leader or aspire to leadership, you need to be able to grasp how they differ.

This understanding can be used as a guide in exercising your leadership. If you simply want to get something done, the authority of your position may suffice. But if you want excellence, you've got to develop the power your fellow workers give you.

Imagine that it's Inauguration Day. When you wake up, you are President of the United States. A few hours later, you are not. Without presidential authority, can you still get things done? Yes — if you have power.

Authority can be conferred, but power must be earned. Without an awareness of this, some managers never develop the power required to lead effectively.

 ## The Nature of Power

What's the one thing a leader must have to be successful?

Followers, right? So basic an answer, and yet it's at the heart of all leadership failures. A leader who has no followers has no power to achieve results.

Unlike an impressive title or a bigger salary, followers can't be awarded to a leader; they must be attracted through honest respect and won by personal effort. We might draw an important distinction here, between appointed leaders and real leaders. You'll see both versions in any organized group: the appointed leader has been given the authority to lead, but it's the real leader who has developed the power to lead.

We all know people for whom we <u>want</u> to do things, and other people for whom we <u>have</u> to do things. Which of these two groups gets our maximum efforts, and which gets the minimum? Those who can inspire us to consistently give our best are the ones with real power. In fact, if a group's real leader and its appointed leader are two different individuals, it's the real leader whom people will more freely follow.

The truth is that power really does come from those who are governed, from their willingness to be led. This suggests to me that successful leadership is really successful followership; it's the ability to earn the respect, support, and involvement of other people who are willing to be guided in a common enterprise. The appointed leaders who don't understand this never fulfill the opportunity of their office. Their designated authority never blossoms into real power, and because they don't have people's respect and support, they eventually lose even that original authority.

Authority without power, after all, is limited in what it can accomplish. For example, if I, as a leader, fail to inspire people to respect me, to want to involve themselves in being led toward a common objective, then there's a point beyond which this company cannot go. If the situation continued long enough, support and confidence would be lost, and eventually – having lost my power to lead – I would soon lose my formal authority as well.

When a leader has been given authority from above and has earned power from below, he or she is in a unique position to help people accomplish great things. True, this combination of power and authority can be hard to handle properly, even for the best-intentioned leaders. (I'd like to offer some observations on that subject in a future letter, "The Temptations of Power".) But when it comes to seeking out candidates for supervisory or managerial positions, I sense a growing awareness in many companies that the people skills of a "real leader" are as important and as desirable as technical skills.

In talking about people skills, I don't mean to suggest that the most popular member of a group is necessarily its real leader. Rather, the individual who really leads others is someone who holds his or her colleagues' respect, and who cares a great deal about helping others to do their best.

In other words, I believe that leadership, too, is based on the mutual respect and caring which are so important to a company's success. It's this respect and caring which are the chief components of power, and which make it such a fragile and awesome force.

The Temptations of Power

"Power tends to corrupt."

Many of us are familiar with that observation, which dates back about a hundred years to Queen Victoria's contemporary, Lord Acton. We all know examples from personal experience that seem to prove the rule... and yet, isn't there something highly ironic about it? In the most recent letter of this series, "The Nature of Power," the conclusion was that power really derives from the consent of the governed; a leader must earn it and hold it by virtue of others' respect for his or her character and capabilities. How can leaders be corrupted by something which others can easily deny them?

The primary opportunity for trouble exists, it seems to me, when formal authority is added to the informal power a leader already exercises – in other words, when a leader becomes aware that if people don't want to follow voluntarily, he or she now has the official clout to make them obey anyhow. It's then that power tends to corrupt, no matter how good the leader's intentions may be, because of the terrific pressure of expectations from above (where the authority comes from) and below (where the power comes from).

The inexperienced leader faces two major temptations: overusing power and authority, and underusing them. Overuse is the more strikingly visible of the two; it springs out of leaders' eagerness to justify their superiors' trust in them, and out of fear of being thought a pushover if they act like nice guys. Symptoms are a tendency to crack the whip constantly, to restrict people's initiative, to take exceptional performance for granted. In essence, this type of leader trades on people's natural desire to cooperate and contribute, without allowing them in return enough of the tangible and intangible rewards of outstanding performance. Eventually, people will lose their willingness to work with individuals like this; and with their real power eroding, these leaders have to fall back on the authority of their office to get results. Once the slide starts, it's hard to stop. Persuasion and involvement are replaced by coercion; people who once gave willingly of their talents and creativity now do the barest minimum of work to get by. For want of a little more consideration and caring, an entire team's effort can be crippled.

On the other hand, there are the leaders who are so considerate of their followers, and so unsure of themselves, that they underuse their power and authority. Knowing that others trust and respect them, they're anxious not to jeopardize their power and risk crushing that spirit of willing cooperation by being tough. What they may not realize, however, is that their reluctance to set and enforce high standards will be perceived by other team members as a lack of caring.

Underuse of power, I believe, can actually cause more problems than overuse, because it leaves people floundering for direction and feedback, depriving them of opportunities to be productive. At first bewildered by the lack of guidance from an individual whom they have confidence in, they eventually perceive that their own growth and the team's progress are being hampered, and their respect for the leader begins to deteriorate. If the leader fails to act at this point, the team can literally disintegrate in front of everyone's eyes.

Power has received a bad name largely because of excesses like these. It's true that much depends on the integrity of those who use it; power in the hands of a Hitler, for instance, is all the more frightening because it was given to him by those he governed. Our first and best defense against villainous leaders is simply common sense. But the majority of leaders would not hold either authority or power if they hadn't started out worthy of trust, and the majority of misuses of power happen through a combination of good intentions and bad judgment.

Note that Lord Acton did not say, as many people think he did, "All power corrupts." He said, "Power <u>tends</u> to corrupt." If leaders can avoid the temptations of power by caring about the people whose effort is vital to the result, as well as caring about the result itself, then there is really no limit to what they can accomplish.

One by One

One way or another, each of us is involved in the challenge to become an excellent human being. It's a vital part of our pride, self-fulfillment, and relationship with others. And when we strive to give our best, one by one we can create a better company together.

Why would anyone rather get lost in the crowd by hiding what they are capable of? "Being average" is a state of stagnation, and it disturbs me greatly that so many individuals are content with it. "Average" may be a passing grade at school, but as a measure of how well a person or company makes use of their potential, it is hardly an achievement. There's no reward for being average, no joy in mediocrity. At best, you succeed in avoiding the penalty for being *below* average. What kind of accomplishment is that?

Just one person can make the difference. One person can start changing attitudes toward excellence, whether he or she is a new employee in a store where slipshod service has become part of the culture, or an accountant in a firm where shady transactions are going on. The affirmation of one good person's behavior tends to make other people instinctively feel good and want to imitate that person's attitude.

Integrity inspires integrity. It's a creative force with a snowballing effect because of the ideals that motivate it. Whether you are promoting from within or hiring new people, it's important to constantly look for individuals who are willing to stand out by being and doing the very best they can.

"Be Thyself"

Fifty-eight years ago, my wife made a sampler that has hung in each of our homes since then. It says, "What you are speaks so loud that I cannot hear what you say."

This simple statement, which I mentioned earlier in the context of leadership, encapsulates everything we tried to communicate in this letter about being yourself. Instead of attempting to make yourself what other people think you should be, concentrate on what you are. Know and understand your own skills, talents, and attributes, and use them to your benefit in what you say, how you look, and where and how you live.

 Be Thyself

Do your associates know the real human being you are – or are you projecting yourself instead the way you think they'd like to see you?

It's so very easy to fall into this trap as a result of the simple desire to impress others. A salesperson who is naturally thoughtful and precise feels it's necessary to project an image as a gung-ho go-getter to impress clients. A worker who, at heart, enjoys her job joins her associates in griping about the boss and the company to impress them with her good fellowship. A supervisor acts like a submissively obedient Dr. Jekyll to impress his superior, then turns into a fire-breathing Mr. Hyde to impress (and intimidate) subordinates.

Imagine: all this role-playing not because we want to, but because we feel somehow it's expected of us! Our lives become controlled by what we think other people want us to be. (And our guesses are usually wrong.)

But you really can't fool all of the people all of the time. Sooner or later, any effort to win respect by impressing people in a phony way will backfire into a loss of respect, once they realize that your appearances don't tally with your actions.

It seems to me far better to act in accordance with your own nature and values, striving to be the same person in the eyes of man that you would like to be in the eyes of God. If you let people see the real you, and do it all the way, be prepared for the fact that you may not be as popular as those who adapt their values easily to what will please others. But instead of approval based on your acting talents, you'll earn a more fundamental kind of respect, as a decent and honest human being.

By being open in this way with yourself and with others, you stand to benefit from one of the greatest rewards of honesty, which is that people will forgive you for being human and genuine. When you're open with others about yourself, they become a little less fearful about revealing themselves as they are. In my experience, honesty generates honesty – and then the chances for effective communication, caring, and respect are tremendously increased.

Please do not read into this message that "anything goes." If you've always tended to be short-tempered under pressure, for example, I'm not suggesting you should feel free to blow your top whenever a deadline looms. Don't stop trying to become the better person which you know you want to be or should be. But the choice of your values and attitudes should come from within, not from what you think other people would like to see.

Knowing you were created as a unique and richly interesting human being, why waste so much of your life fabricating images to mislead people? Be yourself! Stand alone, and let others see the real you.

"A Company of Leaders"

When I left Scotts at the age of 62, after postponing my retirement for two years at ITT's urging, I knew it was the right thing to do. Too many CEOs overstay their peak, well past the point where they can continue giving 100 percent.

At the same time, retiring was the thing I least wanted to do. At Scotts, I truly experienced the joy of work. I had never felt closer to a group of people, and had never before felt the willingness, the acceptance, and the encouragement they gave me to pursue the important subjects in these letters. I continue to miss their fellowship.

In writing this last message, "A Company of Leaders," I tried to sum up the qualities that I hoped would always characterize Scotts Associates and Scotts itself.

 A Company of Leaders

Thank you, my friends and associates, for allowing me to serve you as your leader for the past 16 years. Your trust and willingness to work together with me in this enterprise have brought us to a point which will be the ceiling of my era. Yet before all of you lies the prospect of greater heights of success than Scotts has ever known, for today's ceiling is only the floor of the future.

And thus we've reached the end of the messages. "One Man's Opinion" was never intended to reveal fixed, eternal truths, only personal views of "what can be." I've tried to express through them the values that have guided me as a leader, with the hope that they'll become part of today's benchmark, a starting point for new growth or new directions you may decide to take.

These messages are dedicated to all of you. No matter what the degree of formal authority may be, you are all leaders, dependent on the good will and good work of your associates, influencing each other for better or worse. If nothing else, I hope these thoughts have encouraged you to reach beyond "what is" toward "what can be," by showing you one man's opinion of how you might make it happen.

<u>Be willing to involve yourself emotionally</u>.
Your God-given ability to create things of meaning and value multiplies its effect when you involve yourself wholeheartedly. Enjoy your own creative energy.

<u>Trust others</u>.
The majority of people are fundamentally worthy of trust, and they will respond positively to being respected for their basic honesty and dignity.

<u>Be willing to excel</u>.
Don't hide your high personal standards; share them and inspire others. Make yourself outstanding – visibly outstanding. Leave "footprints" of value in your daily life.

<u>Be considerate</u>.
Remember the importance of other people's willing participation in reaching your goals. Your respect for them can encourage them tremendously; their respect for you makes your success easier to achieve. Communicate clearly and listen clearly.

<u>Be open to new ideas</u>.
Don't avoid them for fear of mistakes. By the same token, learn from your problems; they'll strengthen you as you wrestle with them. Try to control events by acting before they control you. Be courageous!

<u>Last and vitally important: be yourself</u>.
Let other people see the real you. Be as honest with others

as you are with yourself; and don't be afraid to stand up for what you believe in.

Lastly, a personal thank you to each one of you. It has been an unusual privilege to be a part of Scotts and to have had the opportunity to serve you. This is truly a different company with special people. May God bless you individually and collectively.

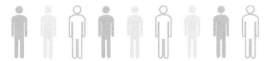

Chapter Nine
Telling Your Company's Story
First, ask the right questions

Chapter 9
Telling Your Company's Story

Every organization has a story.

If you have been stimulated to think about making your own company human, the idea of telling this story may seem daunting. Where does it start? What should it cover? Which developments in your organization's life made it what it is now?

Some leaders may feel comfortable working from the hints and ideas suggested in previous chapters. Others might want more specific guidance — a checklist, for instance.

Checklists are fine for pilots, but they won't do the job here. Companies don't come off a Boeing assembly line. Like human beings, each one is unique.

Asking yourself the right questions

The way you tell your company's story needs to come from your heart. Instead of following a standardized list of topics, you may be able to develop more pertinent and original messages after answering some questions about yourself and your organization.

If you're ready to move forward, we suggest following this three-step process:

Step 1: Identify your personal qualities. What do you stand for? An essential part of making your company human is sharing your own principles, strengths, and aspirations in words and actions. You may be capable of the introspection required for an accurate self-assessment. In many cases, however, you will need to consult someone you trust — a mentor or professional — for help interpreting what kind of person you are. To begin with, how would you answer questions like these?

1. What valuable lessons have you learned, and from whom?

2. Who are your personal heroes? Why do you admire them?

3. Are you logical or emotional? Idealistic or realistic? Flexible or stubborn? If these are not either/or choices for you, why not?

4. What values are sacred to you? Why are they sacred?

5. Have you ever had a serious conflict with a peer or superior on a matter of principle? Why did you take the stand that you did? How was the matter resolved?

6. Are people generally willing to tell you disagreeable truths? Why or why not?

7. Leaders have the opportunity to do things their way. What is (or would be) your way?

8. In your opinion, what is the hardest thing a leader has to do? How would you do it?

9. If you were in the twilight of your career, what would your boss say about you as a person? What would your peer or close advisors say? What about your subordinates? Your friends? Your spouse, if you're married? Your children, if you're a parent? Do they all see you as the same person? If not, what are the differences?

10. Can you be comfortable living the values your company stands for? (Wait to answer this one until you've addressed the next batch of questions.)

Step 2: Define the character of your organization. You have to be clear about yourself before you can be clear about anything else. But you also need to a definite picture of what your company is and what you want it to become. Learn about its past. Find out what it stands for. If the information isn't in plain sight, you may have to work at digging it out. Consider exploring questions like these:

1. What is unique or unusual about your organization's history?

2. What do the people who work there think of it? What do they like and not like? What are they proud of?

3. Do retirees have the same opinion of it as current workers? If not, is it because important things have changed?

4. How is it viewed in the community?

5. Does it have hidden virtues that need to be more widely communicated?

6. Did it at one time have desirable characteristics that it has moved away from?

7. Does it have undesirable qualities that need to be addressed?

8. What business is it really in? How well do your workers understand this?

9. What is unique about the way your organization serves its customers or clientele?

10. What basic emotional need does it try to fulfill?

11. If it has competitors, how does it succeed (or how should it be trying to succeed)?

12. How much do customers trust your company, your brand, or your product?

13. Are you comfortable with the way your company treats customers? Why or why not?

14. Has your organization changed a great deal in recent years? Why or why not?

15. If an opportunity arose to do something radically different, what qualities of the way it does business would be worth protecting?

16. How do your company's people work together?

17. Do corporate practices and policies trust workers to do the right thing?

18. How well do workers know what is expected of them?

19. Are you comfortable with the way workers are treated? Why or why not?

20. If your organization were a person, what kind of person would it be?

21. What should it strive to be, in terms of qualities that people can identify with?

22. What gaps exist between today's reality and the way you would like things to be?

23. Do your own principles mesh with those that are fundamental to your company?

Step 3: Determine the topics to discuss. Based on what you've learned in Steps 1 and 2, you should be in a good position to begin identifying things that workers want and need to hear. For more ideas, it may be helpful to review the subjects of the Scotts letters reproduced in Chapters 7 and 8.

You might first block out broad categories, then pinpoint individual topics in each category. If it feels more natural to do this the other way around — first defining topics, then sorting them into categories — that's fine, too.

You'll also want to decide on the best sequence for introducing the different categories. For example, our "Sharing Some Thoughts" series of letters communicated basic truths about the company. This established a foundation for "One Man's Opinion," the second series, which laid out personal views on important issues. Facts first; then opinions. Reversing the order wouldn't have worked.

A story people are eager to hear

People are the characters in this story. If your company is very large, you may not know who they all are. But what they do is more important. People make things happen. Following their own desires and motives, they create the story.

We all love to hear stories that are about us or our family. That's precisely the kind of tale you have to tell — with all its ups and downs, aspirations and struggles, tribulations and achievements.

It's human nature to want to be a hero, so you may be tempted to mention personal accomplishments or outcomes that make you — directly or indirectly — the star of the story. But that's like moving to the front of the mess line ahead of your hungry troops.

As leaders, we never want to lose sight of the fact that our job is to serve others. They are the true heroes, bringing talent and energy to their work that can help the entire company succeed.

Don't worry about whether they will be indifferent or confused about the letters you send out. If you write from the heart, they'll probably open each new envelope eagerly to read the message you've enclosed.

After all, you're writing about them.

Chapter Ten

The Rewards of Success

The legacy of a leader

Chapter 10
The Rewards of Success

If you asked a dozen ordinary working people to read this book, most of them would probably tell you that there was nothing really new in it. It simply affirmed things that they already felt were right.

Why, then, are these ideas not more widespread in the corporate world?

The overlooked power of human potential

The business community has an opportunity to provide much more of the ethical leadership in this country. Unfortunately, most business schools give their graduates the idea that one need not be a person of high moral substance in order to mobilize and motivate people effectively. But this assumes no distinction between authority and power, between intimidation and inspiration, between fear and joy.

I think every truly effective leader is struggling to be a person of high moral substance. I'm not talking about being perfect, just a fair and decent human being trying to unlock the potential of the people he or she is responsible for.

The B-schools' focus on "doing" instead of "being" results in managers who find it easier to make their numbers by cutting costs or acquiring other companies than by stimulating the talent under their own roof. Most recently, outsourcing to countries with lower labor costs has become a popular way to improve the bottom line. But isn't this a cop-out?

First of all, human needs are the same worldwide. So once these foreign workers feel financially secure, they will ask for the same things domestic workers want — to be treated fairly, trusted, and given meaningful work. A company that outsources to avoid these issues is only postponing the inevitable.

Second, how many organizations have tried going to their own people to see what alternative solutions they can come up with? No matter what the task, inspired people can almost always find a way to do it better.

Leaving a legacy for your company's people

We usually describe businesses in terms of tangibles: products, facilities, customers, and so on. But in companies that defy the norm, like Scotts, it's the intangibles that make the difference. Attitudes, values, ideals — these are what make an organization capable of stimulating the mind and uplifting the spirit.

The letters in Chapters 7 and 8 are an example of how to go about defining, describing, and communicating these intangibles. In the process of setting down your company's heritage and principles, you may help it evolve into something better. As it grows or faces new challenges, people will have a reference point to use in making future decisions. In the event that it considers changing direction, the messages will serve as a record of the course it has attempted to follow thus far.

The benefit of such a program can last for a surprisingly long time. Once established, trust is seldom destroyed overnight. In some of the organizations where abuses have recently taken place, survival may result from a foundation of trust and commitment laid earlier.

The three legs of a strong, stable organization

Most of us want to feel we are an integral part of the company we have joined. But workers are more vulnerable than managers realize. We aren't going to take the risk of stretching ourselves unless the company shows that it is decent, ethical, and serious about treating us fairly.

Fairness is a characteristic I would like to see in every organization — fairness toward workers, customers, and investors. All three groups are important in order for the business to thrive. For example, it's difficult to produce superior goods and services if workers are unhappy, unmotivated, or resentful. Customers are unlikely to come back again if they feel disappointed or cheated. And investors may sell at prices that damage the firm's financial position if they feel the company is not doing well.

CEOs should be compensated on how fairly they serve all three groups. Since we are all human, this may be difficult to achieve. But the more equitably the three groups are treated, the stronger the company will be and the more justifiable the leader's reward. That's the way to build a business.

The rewards of success

Just what is the leader's reward? There is definitely satisfaction in helping the company attain success in terms of market share, market penetration, revenue growth, and so on. Everything in this book is irrelevant if the financial results are not there. When you achieve the intangible result of helping people to open up and contribute their best efforts, it makes these tangible results better and more likely.

For a leader who tries to live in accord with the principles of fairness and serving others, I believe the highest reward is to meet the standard expressed in these words:

A man's no bigger than the way he treats his fellow man.
This standard has his measure been since time itself began.
He's measured not by tithes or creed, high-sounding though they be;
Nor by the gold that's put aside, nor by his sanctity.
He's measured not by social rank, when character's the test,
Nor by his earthly pomp or show, displaying wealth possessed.
He's measured by his justice, right; his fairness at his play;
His squareness in all dealings made; his honest, upright way.
These are his measures, ever near to serve him when they can,
For a man's no bigger than the way he treats his fellow man.
— Author unknown

When I retired, my fellow Scotts Associates presented me with this tribute, "The Measure of a Man." It was the finest reward I could ever hope for as a leader, a validation of the beliefs that have guided me over the years, and the most moving and priceless gift they could possibly have given me.

The effort of making your company human will require you to take your own measure and conscientiously evaluate your deeply held beliefs. If you consider not just what is but what might be, you may be well prepared to unlock the potential of your fellow men and women.

Afterword

A crisis of confidence in American business made me contact Le Herron again.

Some 30 years ago, Le, who was then Chairman, President, and Chief Executive Officer of O.M. Scott & Sons, created a number of unusual letters about the relationship between companies and people. Given the opportunity to help set his ideas down on paper, I was overwhelmed by their simple dignity and humanity. The messages generated a great deal of discussion among the people at Scotts, and inspired a level of pride and enthusiasm that became a high-water mark in many Associates' lives.

The growing distrust of corporate leaders today reminded me of Le's letters and the tremendous power of the concepts they put forth. But after all this time, were his thoughts and ideas still valid?

It was not surprising to find that Le, now retired, had become even more alarmed than I was by the recent waves of fraud and scandal. Faced with an urgent need to address the issue, we began discussing whether a Scotts-type program could help businesses rebuild trust among their workforce.

What evolved from these conversations was broader and more compelling: Le's views on the character of companies and of individuals — especially those who wish to lead. Shaped by good and bad times, and shared with organizations of many sizes and types, these remarkable views have proved their worth.

We hope they will prove helpful as you define your organization's character and shape your own career.

— Sherry Christie

What's behind the cover?

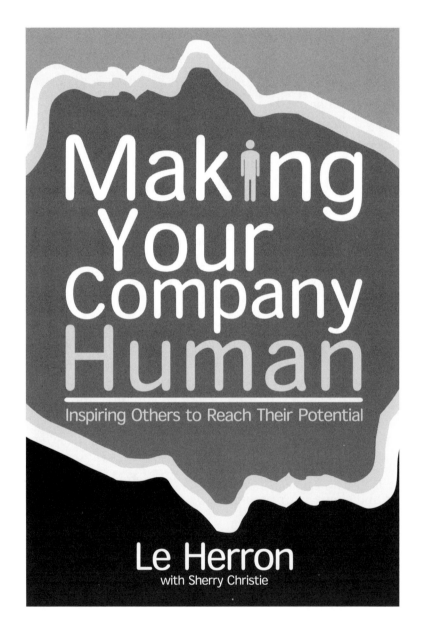

A design for leadership

Making Your Company Human offers readers a tried and true method of inspiring positive change in the workplace — one person at a time.

The result of many years of leadership experience, this book is intended to help aspiring business leaders create an environment that fosters respect, partnership, and individual greatness. It was a labor of love for Le Herron, who infused it with his strong faith and optimism in people's potential.

Once the story was refined and ready to take its place on the page, Le and his associate, Sherry Christie, selected Kernacopia as their creative partner. It was our task to capture Le's vision and reflect his passion through innovative design.

The book jacket makes a bold and contemporary statement, while preserving a degree of classic surrealism. Using varied hues of serene orange and sunset red to reflect Le's own modest, inspiring, and warm personality, it incorporates an abstract profile which is a silhouette of Le himself. As a whole, the design symbolizes his caring personal style, business experience, and timeless philosophy.

The shift in color intensity from cooler to warmer is meant to work on two levels. First, it suggests the one-on-one dialogue between leader and worker that gradually leads to trust and fulfillment. More broadly, it also symbolizes the transformation from a company devoid of individual passion to one that embraces human warmth and a more purposeful existence.

Artwork defining each chapter parallels the cover design, transforming abstract and seemingly intangible ideas into simple icons. Gathering as the story unfolds, the icons multiply through the progression of chapters, suggesting company growth and more complex human connections.

We at Kernacopia have enjoyed the challenge of translating this remarkable story into the book you now hold. We hope you find its messages as inspiring and thought-provoking as we do.

— Kristin Kern, President, Kernacopia, Ltd.

Making Your Company Human would not have been possible without the warmth, wit, and determination of Betty Herron, Le's wife of 58 years (shown here with him and their dog Amanda). Le and Betty live in Marysville, Ohio, not far from their children and grandchildren.